WISCONSIN

WISCONSIN BY ROAD

Apostle Islands
National Lakeshore

Lake
Superior

Superior

Chequamegon

Ashland   Hurley

National

Forest

Chequamegon
National
Forest

Rhinelander   National

Rice
Lake

Timms Hill
(1,951 ft.)

Mohawksin
Lake

Forest

Nicolet

Chippewa
Falls

Wausau

Marinette

River Falls

Eau Claire

Big Eau
Pleine Res.

Green Bay

Marshfield

Black R.

Stevens
Point

Chippewa R.

Wisconsin
Rapids

Petenwell
Lake

Green
Bay

Appleton

Lake
Poygan

Lake
Winnebago

Manitowoc

Tomah

Oshkosh

La Crosse

Castle
Rock
Lake

Fond du
Lac

Sheboygan

Mississippi R.

Wisconsin R.

Beaver
Dam

Lake

Milwaukee

Madison

Waukesha

West Allis

Michigan

Janesville
Beloit

Racine

Kenosha

St. Croix R.

Menominee R.

Green Bay

Wolf R.

CELEBRATE THE STATES
WISCONSIN

Karen Zeinert

BENCHMARK BOOKS

MARSHALL CAVENDISH
NEW YORK

Benchmark Books
Marshall Cavendish Corporation
99 White Plains Road
Tarrytown, New York 10591-9001

Library of Congress Cataloging-in-Publication Data
Zeinert, Karen.
Wisconsin / Karen Zeinert.
p.   cm. — (Celebrate the states ; 3)
Includes bibliographical references and index.
Summary: An overview of the geography, history, people, and customs
of Wisconsin.
ISBN 0-7614-0209-8 (lib. bdg.)
1. Wisconsin—Juvenile literature. [1. Wisconsin.] I. Title. II. Series.
F581.3.Z45   1998   977.5—dc21   96-49381   CIP   AC

Maps and graphics supplied by Oxford Cartographers, Oxford, England

Photo research by Ellen Barrett Dudley and Matthew J. Dudley

Cover photo: *The Image Bank*, Alvis Upitis

The photographs in this book are used by permission and through the courtesy of: *The Image Bank*: Alvis
Upitis, 6-7, 65, 66, 72-73; Gerald Brimacombe, 114; Patti McConville, 138. © *Zane Williams*: 10-11, 13, 17,
18, 20, 22, 23, 52-53, 58 (top and bottom), 68, 76, 78-79, 79 (right), 83, 85, 88-89, 107, 108, 110, 116,
117, 121, 128, 130. *A.B. Sheldon*: 25, 104-105, back cover. *Photo Researchers, Inc.*: Jeff Lepore, 27; Thomas
Hollyman, 119; Tim Davis, 123 (top); Douglas Faulkner, 126. *Milwaukee Arts Museum*: 28-29. *Milwaukee
Public Museum*: 31, 33 (bottom), 34, 37. *National Museum of American Art, Washington, D.C./Art Resource, NY*:
33 (top). *State Historical Society of Wisconsin*: 35, 38 (neg# WHi(X3) 18971), 39 (neg# WHi(X3) 24610), 42
(neg# WHi(X3) 36807), 45 (neg# WHi(X3) 14027), 50 (neg # WHi(X3) 14799), 103. © *John A. Zeinert*: 51,
67, 123 (bottom). *Corbis-Bettmann*: 60, 94, 95. *Fomation*: 70. *John Michael Kohler Arts Center, Sheboygan,
Wis./from the exhibition HMONG ART: TRADITION AND CHANGE, February 24-May 5, 1985*: 78 (left). *Maurice
Thaler, Dane County Cultural Affairs Commission*: 80. *UPI/Corbis-Bettmann*: 82, 93 (left and right), 98, 132 (left
and right), 133, 134 (right). *AP/Wide World Photos*: 87. *The Great Circus Parade, Inc.*: 97. *Oshkosh Public
Museum*: 101. *Wisconsin Department of Administration*: 122. *Reuters/Corbis-Bettmann*: 134 (left).

Printed in Italy

3   5   6   4   2

CONTENTS

INTRODUCTION   WISCONSIN IS . . .   6

1 GEOGRAPHY   THE LAY OF THE LAND   10
SCULPTED BY ICE • SHAPED BY WATER • PLANTS AND ANIMALS ARRIVE • PEOPLE
ENTER THE LAND • FOUR SEASONS TO ENJOY • CARING FOR THE ENVIRONMENT

2 HISTORY   SETTLEMENT TO STATE   28
MOUND BUILDERS • THE FRENCH ARRIVE • THE ENGLISH TAKE CONTROL • AN
AMERICAN TERRITORY • STATEHOOD AT LAST • BUILDING A MODERN STATE •
SONG: "DRIVING SAW-LOGS ON THE PLOVER"

3 GOVERNMENT AND ECONOMY   HOW WISCONSIN WORKS   52
INSIDE GOVERNMENT • CURRENT CONTROVERSIES • EARNING A LIVING •
RECIPE: CHERRY CRISP

4 PEOPLE   WISCONSINITES ARE . . .   72
. . . A RACIAL AND ETHNIC MIX • . . . EAGER TO CELEBRATE • . . . POLITICALLY
UNPREDICTABLE • . . . PATRIOTIC • . . . ENTHUSIASTIC SPORTS FANS

5 ACHIEVEMENTS   LEGENDS IN THEIR TIME   88
PROGRESSIVE THINKERS • ENTERTAINERS • WRITERS • INVENTORS

6 LANDMARKS   "ESCAPE TO WISCONSIN"   104
THE EASTERN LOWLANDS AND RIDGES • THE NORTH WOODS • THE CENTRAL
PLAIN • THE WESTERN UPLANDS

STATE SURVEY   123
STATE IDENTIFICATIONS • SONG • GEOGRAPHY • TIMELINE • ECONOMY •
CALENDAR OF CELEBRATIONS • STATE STARS • TOUR THE STATE • FUN FACTS

FIND OUT MORE   139

INDEX   142

WISCONSIN IS …

People are drawn to this land . . .

"It is so pleasant, so beautifull & fruitfull. The bear, the beaver, and the deer showed themselves to us often . . . indeed it was to us like a terrestrial paradise."

–Pierre Espirit Radisson, French explorer

"This is the finest portion of North America, not only from its soil, but its climate." –Frederick Marryat, English author

It is an impressive "gathering of the waters."
–the meaning of the Indian word *Wee-kan-san*

. . . and they love its astounding wildlife.

"We soon learned to admire the Baltimore oriole and its wonderful hanging nests and the scarlet tanager glowing like fire amid the green leaves." –John Muir, conservationist

"On April nights, when it has become warm enough to sit outdoors, we love to listen to the . . . winnowing of snipe, the hoot of a distant owl, or the clucking of some coot."
–Aldo Leopold, author and conservationist

"We see the wolves' tracks in the snow, hear their howls split the icy stillness of a moonlit January night. . . . It is so satisfying to know that they're here." –Howard Mead, editor

Wisconsinites tend to be a hardy, independent, creative breed . . .

"Cold weather here is something of a loyalty test, and enduring six months of it qualifies one as a local."
–John Hildebrand, teacher

"Wisconsinites collect tales of the coldest, longest, and deepest winters."
–Inga Brynildson Hagge, ecologist

"[They are people] to whom creed, color, race, money mattered less than [anywhere] I've ever encountered."
–Edna Ferber, Wisconsin novelist

"Residents lay claim to the birthplace of the Republican Party, the Burlington Liars Club, and the Ringling Brothers Circus."
–William Curran, writer

. . . with deep-seated enthusiasms.

"They consider former Green Bay Packer coach Vince Lombardi a patron saint."
–Tracy Will, Wisconsin journalist

Wisconsin is the home of five million citizens who are patriotic, politically unpredictable, ethnically mixed, a little feisty at times, and avid sports fans. It is also the home of hardworking people who enjoy their beautiful surroundings and see a bright future ahead. Let's take a closer look at the state and see why Governor Tommy Thompson said that it is "the best state, don't ever forget that."

1 THE LAY OF THE LAND

The area now known as Wisconsin was largely shaped by fire and ice. These powerful forces made dramatic changes in the landscape over a long period of time. About a billion years ago, most of North America, including Wisconsin, was perched on a red-hot mass of molten rock. As this huge mass expanded and pushed upward, it cracked the earth's crust in many places. Molten rock oozed through the openings. When the mass cooled, many new layers were formed. Some of these layers contained iron, copper, or lead.

Then, about one million years ago, the entire area was covered by a huge sea. Many rivers flowed into it and deposited sand. These deposits built up over thousands of years, and eventually, pressure fused the grains of sand in the lowest layers into sandstone.

SCULPTED BY ICE

Very recently in the earth's history, about seventy thousand years ago, four glaciers buried almost half of North America under tons of ice. These glaciers reshaped the landscape as they slid southward.

The last ice field, which began to melt about twelve thousand years ago, covered two-thirds of the present state of Wisconsin. As this glacier moved along, it crushed and compacted the land beneath it and scooped out huge holes, two of which eventually became Lake Superior and Lake Michigan. The ice field also leveled old deposits of molten rock and cut off the tops of ancient mountains. After it had finished its work, the highest point in Wisconsin was less than two thousand feet above sea level. Today this spot is known as Timms Hill. The view from the top is spectacular, espe-

Lake Michigan has sandstone cliffs, sandy beaches, and an abundance of lake trout and whitefish. Many sportsmen would agree with Dan Harris, who says, "The lake is one of the best fishing spots in the Midwest."

cially in the autumn when hundreds of maple trees covering the rolling hills below turn bright yellow, orange, and red.

The last glacier also dropped tons of gravel, soil, and boulders as it moved over the land. And when the glacier finally stopped, it left a huge moraine, a pile of dirt and rocks that had been pushed along in front of the mile-high ice field. Eventually the moraine was covered with vegetation. It is a popular picnic spot.

SHAPED BY WATER

The glacier's effect on Wisconsin's landforms was not limited to what it did while it was solid ice. Nor were its effects seen only in the area that it covered. As the glacier melted, at a rate of approximately one thousand feet per year, water filled Lake Superior and Lake Michigan (which lie along Wisconsin's northern and eastern borders) as well as many of the state's nine thousand or so named lakes, including its largest body of water, Lake Winnebago. (Another six thousand small lakes, mostly in northern Wisconsin, have not been given names.)

Melting water also formed Wisconsin's vast system of rivers, which now totals more than twenty thousand miles in length. The longest of these rivers, the Wisconsin, cuts through the state for more than four hundred miles. These rivers rushed through the new landscape and into the soft sandstone below, where they carved out deep valleys. In the middle of the state, the rivers flowed over flattened areas and created marshlands.

These marshes are very important to Ken Salwey. He is an environmental educator who is determined to protect wetlands. To do

LAND AND WATER

Lake Superior
Superior
Ashland • Hurley

Namekagon R. *L. Chippewa*

Rhinelander

Rice Lake
Mohawksin Lake

Wolf R.
Menominee R.

Chippewa Falls
Wausau
Marinette

St. Croix R.
River Falls • Eau Claire
Chippewa R.
Black R.
Big Eau Pleine Res.
Marshfield
Stevens Point
Green Bay

Wisconsin Rapids
Green Bay

Mississippi R.
Petenwell Lake
Appleton
Lake Winnebago
Manitowoc
Michigan

Tomah
Lake Poygan
Oshkosh
Castle Rock Lake
La Crosse
Fond du Lac
Sheboygan

Beaver Dam
Lake

Wisconsin R.
Madison
Milwaukee
Waukesha
West Allis

Janesville
Racine
Beloit
Kenosha

Mississippi R.

this, he takes people on nature hikes so that they can see a marsh-land's beauty firsthand. "Facts and statistics can only do so much," he says. "The heart and spirit have to be involved in learning to make it last."

PLANTS AND ANIMALS ARRIVE

As soon as the glacier began to melt, plants started to appear. Seeds buried beneath the ice sprouted when they were warmed by the sun. Other seeds were carried into the area by animals or winds. Eventually all of Wisconsin would be carpeted with lush growth.

This growth differed, though, from place to place. The northern third of the state contains two distinct geographic regions: lowlands near Lake Superior, and highlands where the old mountains had been. Both areas have shallow soil and good drainage—perfect places for trees to take root, especially pines. Ferns, fragrant blue violets, and snowy white trilliums sprouted among the trees. Today, both areas are referred to simply as the North Woods. Dotted among the pines are maples, beeches, aspens, birches, oaks, hickories, spruces, and hemlocks.

Once vegetation had taken hold and food and shelter were available, animals began to enter the North Woods in great number. Here the elk, deer, rabbit, squirrel, bear, fox, lynx, marten, and wolf thrived. The streams and lakes teemed with fishes, including twenty-foot-long prehistoric sturgeon and muskies. According to frustrated modern-day fishermen, the clever descendants of these muskies require ten thousand casts before one is caught.

South of the North Woods lies the Central Plain. This area is

Wisconsin's North Woods is dotted with sugar shacks. Here, sap from maple trees is boiled for many hours to create a thick, sweet syrup.

Many snowy egrets live in Wisconsin's marshlands, where, according to Jean Feraca, "it is so quiet, you can sometimes hear a leaf fall."

sandy, flat, and in many places, wet. Tall grasses and bog plants, such as marsh marigolds, lotuses, and wild cranberries, grow here. Prairie grasses and purple asters thrive on the dry land; woods cover the rest.

Animals migrated onto the plain just as they had done in the North Woods. Herds of buffalo wandered across the prairie, and fur-bearing animals sought shelter in the woods and marshes, as did turtles, frogs, sandhill cranes, and trumpeter swans.

Like the North Woods, the southern part of the state is divided into two distinct regions that extend along Wisconsin's western and eastern borders. The glacier stopped in the southeastern section, known as the Eastern Ridges and Lowlands. Where the soil was rich, prairie grasses grew so tall and so thick that they could completely conceal a standing person.

The southwestern section, untouched by any glacier, is now known as the Western Uplands. This area is a dramatic mix of deep river valleys and high sandstone bluffs. Grasses and wildflowers grow in the valleys where cougars and rattlesnakes make their homes. This area is also the home of many birds, including the bald eagle. Each year in January, busloads of birdwatchers head to Prairie du Sac for Eagle Watching Days, both to see the birds and to learn more about them at special lectures sponsored by the city.

PEOPLE ENTER THE LAND

The first people probably came to Wisconsin about twelve thousand years ago, just as the last of the Ice Age glaciers began to melt. Historians know very little about these mysterious people. They do know that they were hunters whose ancestors had come from Asia. Now known as Indians or Native Americans, these nomads followed herds of animals as they migrated across the continent.

As the Indians began to settle in villages, about 7,500 years ago, they chose sites for practical reasons. They settled south of Lake Superior, near Lake Michigan, or along rivers where travel was a little easier. Those who farmed settled in the south, since the long

Dramatic sandstone formations dot the landscape in Wisconsin's Western Uplands.

winters in the north made for a very short growing season. Besides, the soil was better here.

The pattern set by Indians was followed by the white settlers who began to arrive in droves in the 1800s. In fact, this pattern is still followed today. More than two-thirds of Wisconsin's five million people live in the southern third of the state. Four of the state's five largest cities—Milwaukee, Green Bay, Racine, and Kenosha—lie on the shores of Lake Michigan. Madison, the capital, lies in the middle of the state to make it accessible to all residents.

FOUR SEASONS TO ENJOY

The landscape was green and beautiful, but the climate was harsh—and it still is. A northern state in the upper Midwest, Wisconsin has four very distinct seasons.

Summer and winter have the most extreme temperatures. Although a typical July day might be a moderate 70 degrees Fahrenheit, the temperature may on occasion soar to 100 degrees. The average temperature in January is 14 degrees. Spring and fall tend to be more comfortable, but Wisconsinites have to be ready for quick changes in weather. In spring it is not unusual to have warm sunshine, a snowstorm, heavy rains, and blustery winds—all in the same week. Fall is a little more settled, but a sudden burst of snow flurries may appear as early as mid-October.

Wisconsin receives about thirty-five inches of precipitation per year, including melt-off from snow. Parts of northern Wisconsin may get as much as one hundred inches of snow during a really long winter, and snow can stay on the ground in the north for as much as 140 days.

Wisconsinites do complain about the weather, especially when they experience long bouts of bone-chilling winter temperatures that make their ears tingle and their eyes water whenever they step outside. For the Gunderson family of La Crosse, "summer never comes soon enough." On the other hand, a growing number of residents, especially those who like to ski and snowmobile, wish that winter would last even longer. Photographer Jeff Richter loves snow so much that he "can watch it fall all week and not have his fill."

Children often look forward to a heavy snowfall or temperatures

Ice fishing is a popular sport in Wisconsin. Some lakeside cities hold contests, giving awards for the most or the biggest fish caught. Local newspapers carry fishing tips.

dipping to –20 degrees. Travel then becomes so dangerous that schools are closed, giving students a brief vacation. No matter what season a Wisconsinite prefers, few deny that each has its own beauty. A fresh snowfall beneath a bright blue sky in January is quite a sight. And people look forward to wildflower displays in spring, a day at the beach in the summer, and eye-popping color in the fall, when the trees turn brilliant shades of red, orange, and glow-in-the-dark yellow.

CARING FOR THE ENVIRONMENT

Wisconsin's first settlers were awed by the beauty and the wealth of resources that they found there. John Muir, an immigrant from Scotland whose family moved to Wisconsin in 1849 when he was eleven, wrote, "Oh, that glorious Wisconsin wilderness! Everything

Heavy snowfalls can make travel difficult. They also cover the land with a bright white blanket, which contrasts sharply with a brilliant blue sky.

new and pure . . . flowers, animals, the winds and the streams and the sparkling lake."

Unlike Muir, who became one of America's best-known conservationists, many who moved to Wisconsin believed that its resources were so abundant that they would never run out. As a result, too many did too little to protect the environment. Trappers took every fur-bearing animal they could find. When they cleaned out the North Woods, they moved into the marshlands of the Central Plain.

European settlers cleared and plowed under as much flat land as they could to create farms. When they had tilled all the fertile land on the prairie or in the valleys, they dammed up the marshes to prevent rivers from entering them, drained the soil, and tried, unsuccessfully, to farm it. They also cut down forests. This destroyed thousands of acres of wildlife habitat. Meanwhile, loggers felled thousands of trees in the North Woods to satisfy a growing demand for lumber, harming and altering even more of the environment. People everywhere polluted their rivers and lakes, and as manufacturing increased in the cities, the air was filled with soot and foul-smelling fumes.

Fortunately, not all Wisconsinites were willing to see their environment destroyed. As early as 1904, E. M. Griffith, the first man to be hired by the state to protect and expand the state's forests, set out to replant the North Woods. Others followed suit, and to date, fifteen million acres have been replanted. Every year, another twenty-five million trees are added.

The state and federal governments have also stepped in to control protected areas. The first state forest in Wisconsin, Northern

Chequamegon National Forest has many hiking trails, lakes, and streams. Outdoor enthusiasts love its peace and quiet.

Highland-American Legion State Forest, was formed in 1925. It covers 220,000 acres. Today, state forests cover 490,000 acres. The vast majority of these are in the northern part of the state. Two national forests, Chequamegon and Nicolet, stretch over another 850,000 acres in the north.

Aldo Leopold, known as Wisconsin's father of wildlife management, persuaded its citizens to further protect their environment. He began his crusade in 1930 by trying to protect small, unused sites that could support plants and animals. He told Wisconsinites that "There are idle spots on every farm, and every highway is bordered by an idle strip. . . . Keep the cow, plow, and mower out of these idle spots, and . . . native [plants] could be part of the environment of every citizen." People began to follow his advice, setting aside land where plants and animals could live without being disturbed. Some former marshland was flooded and turned over to the federal government for a national refuge. Horicon National Wildlife Refuge, the largest in the state, is about 30,000 acres. It is a nesting area for many waterfowl and a resting spot for more than 250,000 migrating birds each spring and fall. The Necedah National Wildlife Refuge is the home of 700 sandhill cranes.

In addition, residents sought out animals and plants that needed protection. So far, they have identified three mammals, nine fish, two snails, seven reptiles, eleven mollusks, eleven birds, ten insects, and sixty-one plants that are endangered. Anyone who harms these species faces stiff fines.

Now that Wisconsinites have recognized the rare beauty of their state, they are determined to protect and enjoy it. As Wisconsin native Clay Schoenfeld says, "We like the sun coming up over a lake in the morning, and we all notice a good deal about birds. We pay a lot of attention to them. In the silence of a smog-free night, we watch the stars doing their old crisscross journeys in the sky. And we enjoy the change of seasons."

WOLVES, AN ENDANGERED SPECIES

In colonial days, hatred of wolves, which killed livestock, was fanned by vivid accounts about people who supposedly had been attacked and eaten by these daring predators. As a result, many colonies, and later states, offered rewards for any dead wolf that was brought to a bounty station. Wisconsin joined the war, and between 1865 and 1957, the state paid a five-dollar bounty per animal.

In the late 1950s and throughout the 1960s, Americans became more aware of their environment and the important part that each animal played. One of the animals to receive special recognition was the wolf, which was placed on the U.S. Endangered Species List.

To raise awareness and funds to protect all endangered animals and plants in Wisconsin, the state designed a special "Endangered Species" license plate for cars. It features a wolf and any lettering the buyer wants. So far, more than $250,000 has been raised from the sale of these plates. Andrea Benavente, one of the first Wisconsinites to buy such a plate, said, "People give me the thumbs-up when they drive by."

It is unlikely, though, that there will ever again be as many wolves in the state as there were in colonial days. In the 1600s, at least twenty-five thousand wolves lived in the North Woods. Today, there are no more than one hundred.

2 SETTLEMENT TO STATE

Landscape with Palisades along River by Heinrich Vianden

Wisconsin's earliest settlers were Indians who were part of a large culture group that historians now call the tribes of the Northeast Woodlands. They built villages south of Lake Superior. There they found copper in abundance, first in layers of rock close to the earth's surface, and later in veins, which they mined.

These people were craftsmen as well as hunters. They heated chunks of copper over a roaring fire, then pounded the softened metal into spear points and knives. When they had more tools than they could use, they took their surplus to villages around the Great Lakes to exchange for other goods.

MOUND BUILDERS

About A.D. 700, the mound builders arrived. Most of them settled near rivers throughout the southern half of the state. They built more than fifteen thousand earthen mounds, many of which still exist. Some were round or shaped like cones. Most, though, were effigies, built to resemble animals, such as panthers, turtles, and eagles. The mounds were huge. Some eagles, for example, had wingspreads of one thousand feet, and panthers had tails that were three hundred feet long. Historians think that the Indians built the mounds for religious services or burial sites.

Researchers also think that these mound builders were responsible for some impressive rock art in Wisconsin. This includes paintings

An example of early Indian rock art.

(pictographs) on walls in sandstone caves as well as some carvings (petroglyphs) in the stone. The first rock art was discovered in 1878. Since then, ninety-four other examples have been found.

Some of the paintings, illustrations of hunting parties, for instance, are easy to understand. Others contain strange symbols, such as triangles with dots or pairs of wiggly lines that make their meaning a puzzle. Even though we do not understand the entire meaning of this early art, it is important because the Wisconsin samples are one of the largest collections of cave art in the Midwest. Petroglyphs and pictographs can be seen at the State Historical Museum in Madison or at Roche à Cri State Park. Other examples are on private land and open only to researchers.

These Indians were not the only ones to build mounds in Wisconsin. About one thousand years ago, members of the Cahokia tribe, in what is now southern Illinois, migrated to Wisconsin to start a trading village on the Crawfish River. This group, known as the Aztalans, built earthen mounds that resembled Aztec pyramids. Their colony thrived for almost two hundred years before it burned to the ground. According to legend, the Aztalans were cannibals, and their uneasy neighbors finally drove them out. Historians and archaeologists have not completely accepted this story, and they are studying the ruins for more information. Meanwhile, visitors tour the mysterious site, which is now a state park, looking for answers of their own.

At the same time the Aztalans were building their village, other tribes, many of whom were farmers, settled in the southern part of Wisconsin. They raised corn, beans, squash, and tobacco in summer and hunted in winter. The Aztalans were the ancestors of some of the area's modern Indians, such as the Winnebagos.

By the time the first white people entered Wisconsin in the seventeenth century, many Indian tribes were living there. The Chippewa, Sioux, Winnebago, Ottawa, Potawatomi, and Menominee, as well as smaller groups, were spread throughout the land.

THE FRENCH ARRIVE

After North America was discovered by Europeans, several nations sent explorers to the new continent. Among them was France. French explorers quickly realized that North America was extremely rich in fur-bearing animals. Shortly after, they built outposts in the American wilderness, and a thriving trade in pelts between the French and the Indians arose. In search of more pelts, French explorers ventured westward into the wilderness to find more trading partners as well as the fabled water passage to the Far East, where untold riches were to be found.

This scene, which George Catlin painted in 1836, shows Winnebago Indians shooting ducks on the Wisconsin River.

The Menominee Indians were only one of many tribes that lived in the seventeenth century in what is now Wisconsin.

QUILL ART

The Chippewa Indians, also known as the Ojibwa, were a Woodland tribe in northern Wisconsin that became known for their porcupine quillwork, a craft that required both patience and skill. After removing the long, supple quills from the animals—each porcupine has at least thirty thousand—the Indians dyed the quills. They were then worked into baskets and embroidered pieces to add color and create designs.

When other tribes saw the beautiful baskets, they wanted quills of their own. As a result, the Chippewas began to trade quills for other goods. Some of their best customers were Indians from the Great Plains, where porcupines could not be found.

Today, Chippewa Indians continue to give demonstrations of their quill art at special craft shows and powwows held throughout the state. Most quill art, though, is done on five Indian reservations in northern Wisconsin, where more than 7,500 Chippewas live.

This famous painting by Edwin W. Deming shows Jean Nicolet being greeted by Winnebago Indians upon his landing near present-day Green Bay in 1634. A priest who recorded this event said, "He wore a grand robe of China damask, all strewn with flowers and birds of many colors. . . . The women and children fled at the sight of a man who carried thunder in both hands, for thus they called the two pistols that he held."

The best-known French explorer in Wisconsin was Jean Nicolet. He arrived at a narrow body of water (now known as Green Bay) in 1634. Nicolet was most interested in finding the passage to Asia, and he thought that the Indians could help him. But he was afraid that he would not be able to communicate with the natives even though he had Indian interpreters with him. So Nicolet decided to give the Indians a hint of what he was looking for by wearing a silk robe from China. He thought that the Indians would recognize the robe and point out the path that he sought.

Although the Winnebagos who greeted him were greatly impressed with Nicolet and his silk robe, they had no knowledge about a passage to Asia. They tried to offset Nicolet's disappointment by promising to sell pelts to the French. They also held huge banquets for the explorer and his guides, and they invited all the Indians in the area to attend. This was a terrible mistake. Sadly, the French carried diseases for which the Indians had no immunity, and more than half of the Winnebagos became ill and died. French explorers were later accompanied by Jesuit Catholic priests who wanted to convert the Indians to Christianity. Father Claude-Jean Allouez was among the first to reach Wisconsin. He founded several outposts and a rustic mission near the Fox River in 1669. This mission was the site of Wisconsin's first permanent European settlement. It eventually became the city of Green Bay.

Heritage Hill Park, located near the original mission, contains a replica of the first chapel, which was made from bark, as well as replicas of log cabins where the first fur traders lived. Each summer, the park offers demonstrations about life on the Wisconsin frontier. Participants wear authentic costumes, prepare old recipes over wood fires, and display old weapons.

The best-known French priest in Wisconsin was Father Jacques Marquette, who accompanied French explorer Louis Jolliet in 1673. Jolliet was in search of a great river that Indian tribes had often described. The two men and their guides sailed up the Fox

In this painting by George Peter, Father Jacques Marquette and fur trader Louis Jolliet have just come upon the Mississippi River.

River, one of the few in the state to flow northward, until they reached a swampy area and could go no farther. Local Indians then told the French to make a portage, or carry their boats, to the Wisconsin River, which was only a mile away. (Portage, Wisconsin, is located there.)

Once the men reached the river, it was easy for them to sail downstream and into the mighty Mississippi. With the discovery of the Mississippi, the French now had the ability to go from Montreal, Canada, all the way to the Gulf of Mexico almost entirely by water. Marquette recorded the party's great discovery in his journal: "We safely entered Mississippi on the 17th of June, with a joy that I cannot express."

The French built a second settlement at the point where the Wisconsin River joined the Mississippi. This site was called Prairie du Chien ("prairie of dogs," the "dogs" being ground squirrels or prairie dogs). It became an important fur-trading center. The

In 1825, several Indian tribes and the U.S. government negotiated the Treaty of Prairie du Chien. The tribes agreed to give their land to the white settlers.

Fur Trade Museum, housed in one of Wisconsin's best-known mansions, Prairie du Chien's Villa Louis, displays many artifacts from those exciting trading days.

THE ENGLISH TAKE CONTROL

In 1754, France and England began a battle over North America known as the French and Indian War. When it ended in 1763, victorious England got almost all of France's holdings in North America, including Wisconsin.

The British wanted peace with the Indians, most of whom had fought in the war on the side of their trading partners, the French.

The English also wanted to buy pelts from the Indians. To gain both, they decided to stop American colonists from moving into Indian territory by outlawing settlement west of the Appalachian Mountains. This decision greatly upset the colonists and was one of the causes of the Revolutionary War.

AN AMERICAN TERRITORY

The thirteen American colonies won their independence from England in 1783. In addition, they received all the land east of the Mississippi River. Because the western frontier was so far from the East Coast, Wisconsin was ignored for a while, and the French and Indians in the area continued to trade as they had for many years.

However, American settlers began to move into Wisconsin in the early part of the nineteenth century. Some of them were miners.

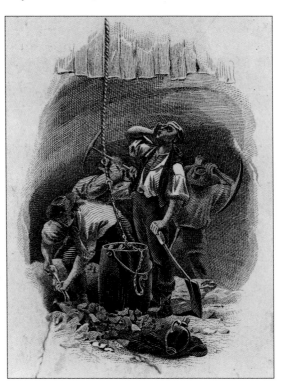

At first, lead in Wisconsin was mined close to the surface of the land. When those deposits were depleted, miners had to go deep into the earth to find the precious metal.

Lead was discovered in 1825 in the southwestern part of the state, at Mineral Point. Word of this find spread quickly, even on the frontier, and miners from Missouri and other areas rushed in to make their fortune. Miners from Cornwall, England, also learned about the discovery, and they, too, made their way to the Wisconsin wilderness. In 1825, there were one hundred miners in the area; by 1828, there were about ten thousand.

The first miners were eager to get to work and unwilling to spend much time building shelters. Instead, they simply dug holes in the ground for homes, covering the openings with boards to keep out the rain. Because these holes were similar to those that badgers dig, the miners were called badgers. Eventually this nickname was applied to all Wisconsinites, and the state became known as the Badger State.

Vast improvements in transportation made Wisconsin easier to reach for would-be badgers. Canals and the invention of the steamboat made it possible to travel by water all the way from New York City to Wisconsin's east coast.

In addition, settling in the state was tempting because of the availability of cheap land. The government bought land from the Indians for as little as $.17 per acre and then sold it to anyone who had the money for $1.25 an acre. This low price made it possible for families to buy large plots for farms and for speculators to buy up whole sections destined to become cities. The result was a land rush. In 1834, there were only two families in what is now Milwaukee. In 1835, there were more than 1,200 people. A journalist noted, "Everyday, almost, new frames [for buildings] were erected."

Winnebago chief Little Elk was amazed at the Americans' determination to own so much land. He said, "The first white man we knew was a Frenchman. . . . He smoked his pipe with us, sang and danced with us . . . but he wanted to buy no land. The [Englishman] came next . . . but never asked us to sell our country to him! Next came the [American] and no sooner had he seen a small portion of our country, than he wished us to sell it *all* to him. . . . Why do you wish to add our small country to yours, already so large?"

Even though Wisconsin's Indians were confused and upset by demands for their land, they seldom argued about selling it. They felt threatened by the white people and the large number of well-armed soldiers who were sent to the territory to protect the settlers. Eventually all of what is Wisconsin would be purchased from the local tribes, who would then live quietly—and in poverty—on the state's eleven reservations.

By 1836, Wisconsin had enough people, a grand population of twenty-two thousand white settlers, to become an official territory of the United States. This area included land west of the Mississippi River, and more than half of the inhabitants lived in what is now Iowa.

Once Wisconsin became a territory, representatives from each county met to form a government. The first legislators held their meetings in inns, which were much like hotels today, until they could build a temporary capital at Belmont. After many heated debates, Madison was chosen as the capital.

Representatives began to press for statehood as soon as the territorial government was established. When Wisconsin became

HENRY DODGE, A COLORFUL CHARACTER

Wisconsin's first territorial governor, Henry Dodge, was a colorful and controversial character. Dodge first arrived in what is now Wisconsin in 1827, where he settled—illegally—on Indian land. He brought with him his wife, nine children, some slaves, and a lot of experience in lead mining that he had gained in Missouri, his home state.

Rumors followed Dodge. He had been charged with being a co-conspirator with Aaron Burr in a treasonous scheme to take control of some of the western states. Dodge was eventually acquitted of this charge, but when it came to light that he had beaten up nine of the jurors when they entered the courtroom, many people wondered if he was truly innocent.

Nevertheless, Dodge became a leader in the lead-mining district in southern Wisconsin near present-day Dodgeville. He organized and headed Wisconsin volunteers in 1832 to capture Black Hawk and a thousand Sauk and Fox Indians. Black Hawk and his followers had returned to Illinois from the West to reclaim their former homeland. Driven out and hotly pursued by an Illinois militia, the Indians fled, attempting to reach safety across the Mississippi River. In doing so, they entered Wisconsin, where they were defeated in a bloody battle at Bad Axe in which Dodge commanded the troops. From then on, he was regarded as a hero, and he was appointed territorial governor in 1836.

Dodge was not a typical governor. He always carried a Bowie knife and often used foul language, which shocked ladies and even some gentlemen. Still, Dodge was an able governor, leading the first government in the territory and overseeing the committees that were selected to write a constitution. He also represented Wisconsin in the U.S. Senate from 1848 to 1857.

a state, it could receive financial help from the federal government for internal improvements such as roads, railroads, and canals. Before all that could happen, though, it had to have sixty thousand residents.

To reach the necessary number as soon as possible, recruiters set out to convince people to move to Wisconsin. They traveled to the East Coast and Europe, promising cheap land and a good living. They were so successful that by 1848 Wisconsin had more than two hundred thousand people. Six years later, the population had doubled, an amazing rate of growth. The new Wisconsinites came from nearby states, such as Missouri and Illinois, as well as many eastern ones, especially New York. Settlers also came from overseas, from Germany, England, Ireland, Norway, Finland, and Switzerland. In the years to come, they would be joined by Italians, Poles, Czechs, and many more Germans.

Immigrants often wrote letters to friends and family members in their homelands to encourage them to move to Wisconsin. Among them was George Adam Fromader, from Germany, who settled in Jefferson City in 1847. His first letter to friends was filled with encouragement and advice:

> Anyone who has a desire to follow us may do so confidently if he can bring a little money along, whether it be a father or a family or a single person, man or woman. A skilled and industrious woman even though she brings no money into the country [for a dowry] may soon become a housewife. Women are highly respected in this country. . . . Whoever wants to make the trip need not bring a great deal except a supply of shirts and woolens. Do not bring tools of any kind, nor extra shoes, for the German ones are not worth carrying across the sea. No matter what you need or want, it is much better [here] than in Germany. The best route, also the cheapest, is via Bremen [a German port] and New York. The provisions to take on the trip are: good rye bread, cut small and toasted, oatmeal fried in lard, dried pork, dried noodles, coffee and sugar . . . , dried prunes, salted butter, white hard tack. . . . You have no need for more advice, for I have told you all that is necessary.

Wisconsin's immigrants brought with them strong skills and a great desire to work. They were farmers, mechanics, craftsmen, teachers, traders, preachers, and politicians. All of them had something to offer, and all of them believed they were equal to the tasks before them and as good as their neighbors.

STATEHOOD AT LAST

In 1846, with more than the necessary sixty thousand residents, representatives from the territory asked the federal government to make Wisconsin a state. Congress agreed to do so, and on May 29, 1848, Wisconsin became the thirtieth state in the Union.

Wisconsin's representatives did not receive control over as much land as they had hoped. Lakes Superior and Michigan made natural borders for the state on the north and east. Since borders for Michigan and Illinois had already been drawn years before, when those states entered the Union, Wisconsin could only lay

Farmland in Wisconsin was—and still is—rich. This family purchased land in 1880. Fifteen years later, they had acquired enough money to build a fine wooden house (shown in the right of the photo), complete with glass windows.

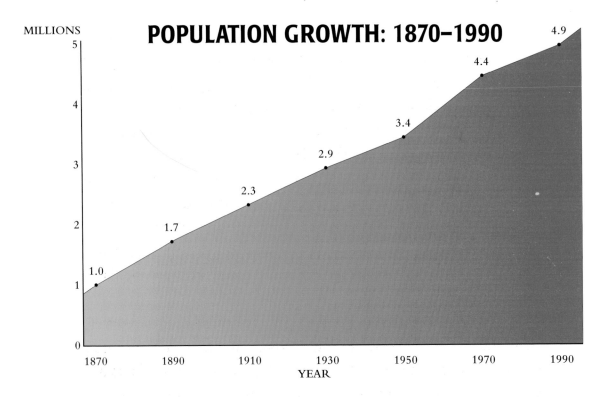

POPULATION GROWTH: 1870–1990

MILLIONS

5 — 1.0

4

3

2

1

0

1870   1890   1910   1930   1950   1970   1990

YEAR

claim to what is Wisconsin today, plus land beyond the current western border. But the federal government decided to use the natural boundaries of the St. Croix and Mississippi Rivers for the state's western edge, eliminating all Wisconsin claims to what would become Minnesota and Iowa. As a result, Wisconsin was limited to fifty-six thousand square miles.

BUILDING A MODERN STATE

The limit on land did not limit Wisconsinites' desire to build a prosperous state. In fact, they set about their goal with even greater determination. One visitor from Ohio was amazed at the activity he saw in Milwaukee. He wrote, "A fellow can hardly get along the sidewalk. . . . Every kind of mechanism is going on in this place, from street hawking to manufacturing steam engines."

Meanwhile, farmers began to consider raising larger dairy herds. Wheat was the major crop then, but it wore out the soil quickly. And because it needed a long growing period, it could only be raised in the southern part of the state. On the other hand, feed for cattle, primarily grass, grew all over the state. When the first cheese factory was built in Ladoga in 1864, it was very successful. Farmers then abandoned the plow for the cow, and a thriving dairy business was born.

To help farmers and businesses get their products to market, state officials led the drive for better roads and new railroad lines. By the end of the nineteenth century, Wisconsin had six thousand miles of railroad tracks. That made it possible for businesses to exist almost anywhere, and Wisconsinites—two million strong— fanned out across the state.

Many of the new businesses made wooden products from the tall pines harvested in the North Woods. By 1900, Wisconsin led the country in the manufacture of wooden doors and wagons. The state would later become a major producer of wood pulp and paper products.

Although growth has always been a major goal in the state, many Wisconsinites are no longer eager for more development. They worry that more industry and sprawling suburbs will harm their environment. Door County has already decided to limit growth. Says one county representative, "The time for action is now, while

DRIVING SAW-LOGS ON THE PLOVER

Loggers were known as shanty boys because the cabins they lived in were called shanties. In this song the mother of a shanty boy is trying to discourage her son from continuing in this dangerous occupation. Surprisingly, he takes her advice. By the last verse he is telling other would-be shanty boys to stay at home on the farm.

There— walked on Plo-ver's shad-y banks one eve-ning last Ju-ly,— A moth-er of a shan-ty boy, and dole-ful was her cry.— Say-ing,"God be with you, John-nie, al-though you're far a-way,— Driv-ing saw-logs on the Plo-ver, and you'll nev-er get your pay".—

O Johnnie, I gave you schooling,
I gave you a trade likewise;
You need not been a shanty-boy
Had you taken my advice.
You need not gone from your dear home
To the forest far away,
Driving saw-logs on the Plover,
And you'll never get your pay.

O Johnnie, you were your father's hope,
Your mother's only joy.
Why is it that you ramble so,
My own, my darling boy?
What could induce you, Johnnie,
From your own dear home to stray,
Driving saw-logs on the Plover?
And you'll never get your pay.

Why didn't you stay upon the farm,
And feed ducks and hens.
And drive the pigs and sheep each night
And put them in their pens?
Far better for you to help your dad
To cut his corn and hay
Than to drive saw-logs on the Plover,
And you'll never get your pay."

A log canoe came floating
Adown the quiet stream.
As peacefully it glided
As some young lover's dream.
A youth crept out upon the bank
And thus to her did say,
"Dear mother, I have jumped the game,
And I haven't got my pay.

"The boys called me a sucker
And a son-of-a-gun to boot.
I said to myself, 'O Johnnie,
It is time for you to scoot.'
I stole a canoe and started
Upon my weary way.
And now I have got home again,
But nary a cent of pay.

"Now all young men take this advice;
If e'er you wish to roam,
Be sure and kiss your mothers
Before you leave your home.
You had better work upon a farm
For half a dollar a day
Than to drive saw-logs on the Plover,
And you'll never get your pay."

the county still has its charm." Two other counties in the state have followed suit. As the twenty-first century dawns, Wisconsonites, like people everywhere, will be weighing the value of industrial development against the desire to preserve their much-loved land.

In Wisconsin's forests grew huge pine trees, many of which were cut down when the demand for wood soared in the late nineteenth century.

Today, it is not unusual to see housing developments right next to farms, especially near large cities. Some residents, like Norbert Blei, consider developments "a blight on the land."

3 HOW WISCONSIN WORKS

The state capitol in Madison

For a territory to become a state, it had to have a constitution, and Wisconsin was no exception. But Wisconsin's constitutional committee faced an especially difficult task. Imagine trying to write a constitution that would satisfy many different ethnic groups, some of whom could not speak to each other because they did not have a common language! Also, imagine trying to design a state government that would be strong enough to hold these groups together, settle disputes when they arose, and provide a way to let people govern themselves on a local level so that their specific needs could be met.

INSIDE GOVERNMENT

The constitutional committee set out to meet this challenge by organizing the state government. It is still much as it was in 1848, with three branches: the legislative, the executive, and the judicial.

Legislative. The legislative branch has two bodies, the senate and the assembly. The state is divided into thirty-three districts by population, and citizens in each district elect one member to the state senate and three representatives to the assembly. The legislature drafts bills that become law if they pass both bodies and are signed by the governor. It also decides how taxes are generated and how they are spent.

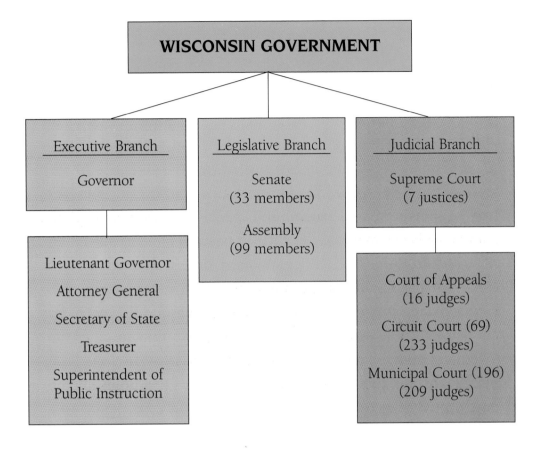

Executive. The executive branch is headed by a governor. This branch has other officers as well: a lieutenant governor, an attorney general, a state treasurer, a secretary of state, and a superintendent of public instruction. All of these officers are chosen by voters in statewide elections. Rarely are all of them from the same political party. As a result, political clashes in the executive branch are not unusual, and its leaders become feisty at times.

Executive officials have two jobs. They make sure that the state's laws are executed, or carried out. They are also responsible for identifying problems in schools, society, or the economy, for which they are to find solutions—no small task.

Judicial. The judicial branch tries people accused of crimes and settles disputes. This branch consists of three kinds of courts: circuit courts, courts of appeal, and a supreme court. The sixty-nine circuit courts are the first to hear cases. The court of appeals listens to pleas from people who have lost their cases in circuit court. The Wisconsin Supreme Court is the court of last resort; it hears pleas from people who have lost their first appeal if it believes that justice might not have been done. This court has seven justices. In 1997, it was headed by Justice Shirley Abrahamson, the first woman to be chief justice.

Judges are elected in Wisconsin. Circuit court and appeals judges are chosen in the district in which they serve, and supreme court justices are selected in statewide elections. Unlike other elected state officials, judges may not campaign as members of a political party, nor can they discuss how they would vote on a particular issue should it come before the court. Voters are to select judges based on their ability to make good decisions, not on their beliefs.

CURRENT CONTROVERSIES

Wisconsin's government works well. Even so, the state has problems to solve. Currently, education, the death penalty, and Native American rights receive the most attention.

Education. Wisconsin's first public schools opened their doors in 1848, the year Wisconsin became a state. By 1879, all children were required to go to school through eighth grade.

Today, students must remain in school until they graduate from high school or reach their eighteenth birthday. The only ones who are exempt from this law are the Amish, members of a religion that rejects all modern inventions, even electricity. The number of Amish is growing in the state, especially in the central and western counties. Amish children leave school when they have finished their basic education in eighth grade.

The first German immigrants to arrive in Wisconsin brought with them a tradition of private education. Some of these immigrants started their own schools, and they established the first kindergarten in the United States. Other Wisconsinites started private schools as well, most of which were run by Protestant churches or

MARGARETHE SCHURZ'S KINDERGARTEN

In 1852, Margarethe Schurz and her husband, Carl, left Germany for the United States, where they first settled on the East Coast. They soon decided to move westward. They chose Wisconsin as their destination, and in 1856, they arrived in Watertown, a small town in the southern part of the state.

While Carl busied himself with political issues, Margarethe turned her attention to children, whom she loved dearly. She decided to open a school for four and five year olds, which was based on schools that she had observed in Germany. Margarethe called her school "kindergarten" ("garden of children"). Schurz taught her students to socialize, sing, dance, and play games to make their introduction to schooling as pleasant as possible. The idea of having kindergarten caught on, and today almost all school systems offer this class.

The number of Amish in Wisconsin is growing. Girls are taught how to make quilts—twelve stitches to the inch—when they enter their teens.

More than nine hundred thousand children attend school in Wisconsin. In addition to the basics, they learn about the state's environment and how to protect it.

Catholic parishes. Today, about 150,000 Wisconsinites attend private elementary or secondary schools, while 900,000 go to public schools.

Local school districts control the public schools. Most of the money that funds these schools comes from local property taxes. Because wealthy districts can afford better buildings, more up-to-date textbooks, more computers, and more teachers, differences among school systems have widened over the years. Parents in some of the poorer districts have been very upset with the schools when their children score poorly on standardized tests. However, many cannot afford to send their sons and daughters to private schools.

In response, Governor Tommy G. Thompson and members of the state legislature proposed a pilot program in 1990 to help parents pay tuition costs in Milwaukee's private schools, including several that are run by religious organizations.

Supporters of public education were deeply upset with Thompson's plan for a number of reasons, including the belief that it violated the U.S. Constitution's prohibition of government support for religion. These men and women challenged the program in court, and by doing so, put the program on hold. None of the courts have supported Thompson's plan. Whether the last decision, announced in January 1997, will be appealed by school choice advocates is unknown.

Meanwhile, some parents who assumed that the courts would support the plan put their children in private schools. Now they are struggling to keep their children there. Pilar Gonzalez has taken on an additional job so that she can pay tuition for her children,

Governor Tommy Thompson supports school choice. He also wants higher standards in education and says he plans "to have a graduation test in place by 1999."

ages seven and nine. "It's kind of heart wrenching—whether to continue keeping my children in private education or risk putting them back in public education," she said.

The Death Penalty. The crime rate in Wisconsin is quite low. The state ranks in the lower third of all states for all crimes and is number forty-one for violent crime. However, several especially brutal murders of children have so angered and upset Wisconsinites that instituting the death penalty for murder is now being considered. Rick Jones, whose twelve-year-old daughter, Cora, was murdered, supports the death penalty. He said, "I think people who kill . . . ought to be put to death. I think that it might restore some sense of faith in the justice system."

State Senator Alan Lasee also supports the death penalty. He says that murderers lead too pleasant a life in Wisconsin prisons, working, taking classes, and eating treats such as brownies. "That's what you get for murdering another human being," he thundered at a 1996 hearing on the death penalty. "Whatever happened to bread and water? Whatever happened to breaking rocks with a sledgehammer? Whatever happened to the death penalty?"

Opponents argue that the death penalty is just another form of murder. Reverend Paul Martin, who believes that killing criminals is wrong, said that if Wisconsinites execute criminals, "We're doing the same thing we're angry about."

Don Gabrilska is against the death penalty because he believes that it will not be applied equally: "I feel only the poor will get executed. The rich don't get convicted anymore."

Because this is such an emotional issue—and therefore politically risky—some legislators want Wisconsin's citizens to decide if the state should have a death penalty. They hope to put the question to a statewide vote in the near future.

Native American Rights. The question of Native American rights is also dividing the state. When Indians sold their land, the state gave them permission to hunt and fish without limit on public lands and lakes. In recent years, this has caused great controversy.

Some of the tribes have decided to take what is considered 100 percent of the safe harvest in certain lakes. In 1996, for example, the Chippewa declared that they intended to spear 54,000 walleyed pike. In order to accomplish this goal, the Chippewa would have had to take the allowable harvest in seventy-nine lakes in northern Wisconsin, closing them to non-native fishermen for at least one year. Resort owners who make their living from tourists who love to fish were understandably very upset. So, too, were local fishermen.

State officials were furious. Darrell Bazzell, speaking for the governor, said, "We are extremely angry with the [tribe's announcement]. . . . Unless it is changed, without doubt, [it] will set back the relationship between Indians and non-Indians in this state for years to come."

Opponents of the Chippewa plan fought back by threatening to boycott very successful gambling operations on Indian reservations, which have greatly improved tribal lifestyles in the last twenty years. Shortly after, a temporary compromise was worked out: The Chippewa agreed to take fewer pike. However, since tribes still have the right to harvest whatever they wish, the conflict is far from over.

EARNING A LIVING

Most workers in Wisconsin are employed in agriculture, manufacturing, and the service sector, which includes trade and tourism. About three hundred thousand people work for the government. The state economy continues to grow each year and provides many job opportunities, especially in or near the largest cities. In 1996, the average income per person was $25,099. This was below the national average of $27,845. However, Wisconsin's unemployment rate for that year of about 3 percent was also well below the national average.

GROSS STATE PRODUCT: $156 BILLION

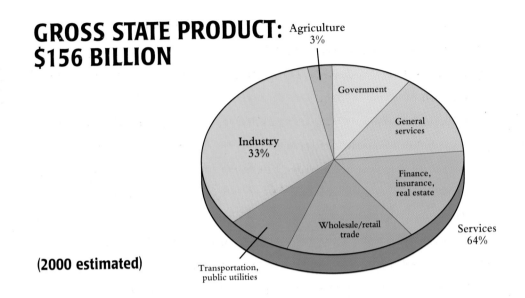

Agriculture
3%

Government

General
services

Industry
33%

Finance,
insurance,
real estate

Wholesale/retail
trade

Services
64%

(2000 estimated)

Transportation,
public utilities

Agriculture. There are about seventy-nine thousand farms in Wisconsin, with an average size of two hundred acres. Even though farmers and the people they hire make up only a small percentage of the state's workforce of 2.5 million people, they produce many crops and have a significant effect on the economy, producing commodities worth $10 billion each year.

Today there are 1.5 million cows in the state, which produce 3 billion gallons of milk annually—enough to furnish every American with a quart of milk every week! But not all of this milk is used as a beverage. Some of it is turned into butter and cheese and other dairy products. Wisconsin ranks first among the states in the production of cheese and second in the production of milk and butter. That's why Wisconsin is often called America's Dairyland.

Jeff Pollack is a young, successful dairy farmer. His 365 cows provide 24,000 pounds of milk each day. Pollack is very optimistic

EARNING A LIVING

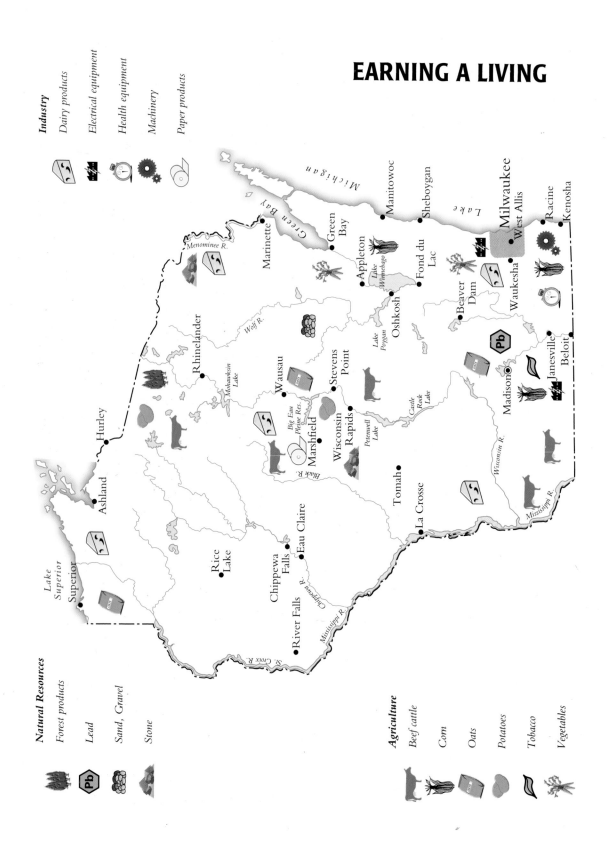

Industry
- Dairy products
- Electrical equipment
- Health equipment
- Machinery
- Paper products

Natural Resources
- Forest products
- Lead
- Sand, Gravel
- Stone

Agriculture
- Beef cattle
- Corn
- Oats
- Potatoes
- Tobacco
- Vegetables

Wisconsin farms are home to more than one million cows, which produce three billion gallons of milk each year. Governor Thompson believes that the state's farms will produce even more in the future.

about the future. "Dairy farming is in good shape," he said. "Things are looking up. Our cheese could go up against any. A lot of places don't have good quality cheese. If we can get our cheese out there, it will play an important part in increasing dairy-product sales."

Wisconsin's farms lead the nation in the production of snap beans, peas, beets, and cranberries, as well. It is also one of the

Wisconsin cheese is world famous. Here, cheesemakers are forming blocks of mozzarella from fresh curd. Mozzarella is often used in pizza.

top producers of sweet corn, cucumbers for pickles, cabbage for sauerkraut, and potatoes for chips and frozen fries. Other farm products include maple syrup, honey, apples, and cherries as well as beef cattle, hogs, and chickens.

Perhaps the state's most unusual farm product is ginseng. This root crop is in great demand in the Far East, where it is used in medications. Ginseng is a fussy plant that is difficult to grow; it needs acidic soil, light shade, and perfect drainage. It also grows slowly, requiring at least five years of cultivation before it can be harvested. However, ginseng root sells for fifty dollars a pound in Asia. Wisconsin's Marathon County, in the middle of the state, is the

CHERRY CRISP

Cherries have been an important ingredient in eastern-Wisconsin dishes for many years. Below is a simple recipe for a scrumptious dessert called cherry crisp.

Crust:

1 stick of butter, melted
1 cup brown sugar, packed down
1 cup flour
1 cup quick-cooking oatmeal
¼ teaspoon each baking powder, salt, and baking soda
sprinkling of cinnamon

Filling:

2 cups pitted tart cherries (fresh or frozen, thawed, drained)
¾ cup cherry juice or water
¼ to ½ cup sugar (sweeten to taste)
3 tablespoons cornstarch
⅛ teaspoon almond extract

Mix all ingredients for crust except cinnamon. Pat half of this mixture into a 9 x 9 x 2 inch pan. Blend cornstarch, sugar, and liquid in saucepan over medium heat. Bring contents to a boil, then simmer, stirring constantly, until mixture thickens. (Ask an adult to help you.) Add extract and cherries. Pour filling over crust. Sprinkle the remaining crust mixture over the filling. Top with a sprinkling of cinnamon. Bake in a 350° F oven for 30 to 35 minutes. Serve warm or cold, with or without vanilla ice cream.

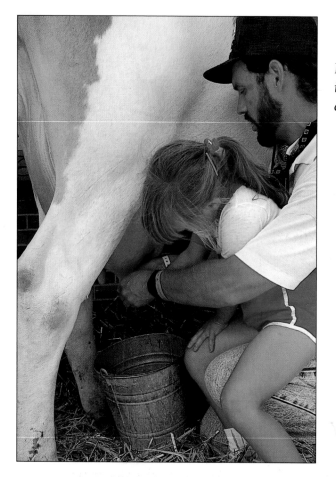

Demonstrations at the state fair include a lesson on how to milk a cow.

world's leading ginseng producer. One farmer recently harvested more than three hundred thousand pounds!

The best of Wisconsin's agricultural products are put on display at the state fair, held each year in Milwaukee. Fairgoers often begin their day by examining produce-laden tables holding the biggest tomatoes, the reddest homemade strawberry jam, and the tastiest cherry pie. They then head to the barns to see some of the best calves, pigs, sheep, geese, ducks, and rabbits in the state, most of which were raised by children. Fairgoers also watch tractor pulls and horseback-riding competitions. And they sample freshly roasted corn-on-the-cob and as many rich cream puffs—a fair specialty—as their waistbands will allow.

Industry. More than 580,000 Wisconsinites work in manufacturing firms. Ninety-five percent of these companies employ fewer than fifty people. They make products from local raw materials or from imported goods, which are often shipped into one of the ports on Lake Michigan. Altogether, Wisconsinites manufacture products worth more than $36 billion each year. Among the best known are Oshkosh B'Gosh clothing, Oscar Mayer hot dogs, Frito-Lay snacks, J. I. Case tractors, John Deere snowmobiles, Mercury outboard motors, Harley-Davidson motorcycles, Ray-o-Vac batteries, paper products such as Kleenex, submarines for the government, and yachts for the wealthy.

Perhaps one of the best-loved products, though, is manufactured by a company that has only five employees: Foamation makes funny foam hats shaped like a wedge of cheese for sports fans. Chris Becker, the general manager of the company, says that he has shipped "cheeseheads" all over. "We've had calls from Germany, Japan, and the Netherlands." Sue LeMay, a receptionist who has handled many requests for the product, adds, "People are just fascinated with these cheeseheads."

The Service Sector. The service sector is the largest employer in the state. About 450,000 Wisconsinites earn their living by selling Wisconsin products or imports to the public. Another 40,000 workers are employed by trucking and warehousing firms, which transport and store these goods. Other service businesses include banks, real estate, insurance and communications companies, restaurants, hotels, hospitals, and the tourism industry.

One of Wisconsin's best-known products is the cheesehead. Green Bay Packer fans, who wear them to football games, have made the hats world famous.

About ten million tourists visit Wisconsin annually. For most of these visitors, the outdoors is the great attraction. They camp in one of Wisconsin's forty-four state parks, hike state trails, bike country roads, catch some of the sixty million fish taken yearly from state waters, ski, snowmobile, hunt, shop, and relax. In the process, they spend $6 billion a year in the state. To encourage even more tourists to visit, Wisconsin has adopted the slogan "Escape to Wisconsin!" as the theme of an advertising campaign that is seen across the nation.

But not all popular tourist destinations are encouraging more visitors to come. Residents of one northern county here decided against building more motels for the increasing number of visitors clamoring to get in. Bob Hastings, a spokesman for the county, was hesitant to announce the group's decision, fearing a backlash. To his surprise, he has received tremendous support. "Overwhelmingly positive doesn't begin to describe the response," he said.

4 WISCONSINITES ARE...

Wisconsinites come from many different places and hold a wide array of beliefs. It is not easy to describe a typical resident. Still, some generalizations can be made. They are . . .

. . . A RACIAL AND ETHNIC MIX

In the first part of the nineteenth century, most people in Wisconsin were Native American. That has changed dramatically over the years. Today, out of a total population of 5 million, only 50,000 are Native American. Approximately 4,600,000 are white, 250,000 are black, and 100,000 are Asian. Half of the state's Asians are Hmongs, an ethnic group from Laos that actively supported the United States during the Vietnam War. The Hmongs were forced to flee their homeland when the United States withdrew from Asia at the end of the Vietnam War. Wisconsin is home to one of the country's largest concentrations of Hmongs.

Although only 2 percent of Wisconsinites are Hispanic, their number is growing faster than that of any other group. Some of them are former migrant workers who decided to stay after going to Wisconsin to help harvest farm crops.

. . . EAGER TO CELEBRATE

Wisconsinites love to celebrate, and they hold festivals to honor the many ethnic groups that live in the state. They also get together to celebrate at harvesttime. And if they want to host a party but lack a special reason, they invent one. As a result, Wisconsin has some rather unique events, including a cherry-pit spitting contest in Fish Creek.

German Fest, the largest festival of its kind in North America, is held in Milwaukee in the summer. Bands play polkas, craftspeople demonstrate Old World skills, and workers in food tents struggle to keep up with the demands for wurst (sausage), soft pretzels (similar to soft breadsticks), and beer. These three days of singing and dancing and fellowship are called *Gemütlichkeit* in German.

ETHNIC WISCONSIN

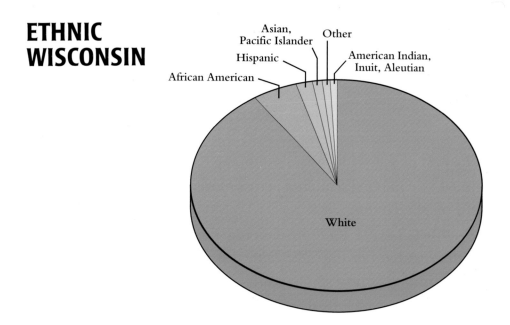

African American
Hispanic
Asian, Pacific Islander
Other
American Indian, Inuit, Aleutian
White

Many ethnic groups hold festivals. Singing, dancing, craft displays, and tasty treats are among the many highlights in celebrations, which often last for several days.

Instead of statewide festivals, Hmong communities hold smaller annual celebrations scattered across Wisconsin. Most of these are held on the Hmong New Year, which usually falls at the end of November. Events include dancing demonstrations by young children, guitar playing, and games, such as *pov bob*, a ball game played among young single adults as part of a courtship ritual. Usually, festivals include displays of women's intricate needlework.

These include appliqué, delicate beadwork, and hundreds of tiny decorative stitches. Many needlework projects are quilts that picture Hmong villages or illustrate an historical event.

The number of Hmong participants and visitors grows every year. More than two thousand people attended a recent celebration in Oshkosh. Organizers, such as Ying Lee, are pleased with the increased interest in their culture, especially among children. Their participation, according to another festival organizer, Deborah Skowronski, is vital. She said, "Children are an integral part of keeping cultural traditions alive."

Various Native American tribes also host festivals—powwows—in Wisconsin. Thirteen-year-old Thirza Defoe, an Oneida Indian, performs in many of these celebrations. Part of her demonstration includes a traditional hoop dance, during which she uses sixteen hoops at one time. She learned how to do this dance in an Indian school in Milwaukee.

Thirza is eager to educate other Wisconsinites about Native cultures. "Sometimes when I dance," she said, "non-Indians come around and make fun of me with those 'whoo-whoo' war cries they see in movies. It makes me mad because they should know better." She often takes these people aside to talk to them. She explains her customs and shows them that she is just a normal teenager.

Not all celebrations are ethnic in nature, though. Wisconsinites love to eat, and they often celebrate when crops are harvested. There are so many of these festivals that it is hard to keep track of them all. Terese Allen toured the state while writing a book about the state's food festivals. She has identified two hundred fifty so far!

Several Indian tribes host powwows in the summer.

The Hmong are some of the latest immigrants to arrive in Wisconsin.

Every winter, New Glarus, a village with a Swiss heritage, hosts a unique festival. Villagers build huge bonfires and blow their alpenhorns to "kill" winter and bring an early spring.

ROSEMALING

Wisconsin's many ethnic festivals often showcase special crafts. Norwegian celebrations feature rosemaling. It is an old art of decorating wooden objects with vivid designs, which include painted flowers, leaves, and scrolls.

Hundreds of years ago, some artists in Norway made a living by traveling from home to home, decorating cupboards and wooden chests. The designs were often unique to a particular area or valley, and art experts today can tell where the artist came from by examining the design. Although rosemaling flourished for many years, it went out of style in the late nineteenth century.

Interest in the craft was revived in Wisconsin by Per Lysne of Stoughton. Lysne had long admired old rosemaling designs, and he set out to duplicate them in the 1930s. He began by decorating some wooden plates and cupboards for friends. Word of his artistic ability spread, and soon others were asking him to do some work for them. As more and more people saw Lysne's designs, they became interested not only in the artist but in the art itself. As a result, others took up rosemaling. Today, several community colleges offer classes in this ethnic craft.

She knew about the strawberry, apple, cherry, and mustard festivals. "But," she added, "I was amazed to learn we have celebrations that feature rutabagas, sauerkraut, bluegills, ginseng, and pea soup."

. . . POLITICALLY UNPREDICTABLE

Although Wisconsinites can be expected to attend festivals in huge numbers, when it comes to voting they are unpredictable. They do not consistently support any one political party over another. They might elect a Republican governor and a majority of Democratic representatives to the state assembly. On the other hand, they have been known to repeatedly reelect candidates they like. Governor Tommy Thompson, a Republican, has served three terms in office, and is running for a fourth. Senator Gaylord Nelson served in the U.S. Senate for eighteen years, between 1963 and 1981. Before that, he was governor of Wisconsin.

Over the years, Wisconsinites have elected representatives of very different political beliefs. In the early nineteen hundreds, Wisconsinites supported candidates known as Progressives, who promised to change government and make it more responsive to the people. Government, they believed, could solve problems.

By the middle part of the century, many Wisconsinites no longer trusted political leaders, especially on the federal level. They believed that government not only couldn't solve problems, it had become a problem in itself. Full of doubt and mistrust, the voters sent Joseph McCarthy, a new man to the political scene, to the U.S. Senate in 1947.

Joe McCarthy's search for communist spies employed by the federal government began in 1950.

McCarthy became one of the state's most controversial senators. He believed that the federal government had been infiltrated by communist spies who were plotting to destroy the country. He set out—with a vengeance!—to expose them. When Americans cheered him on, McCarthy, who was politically ambitious, made many accusations. "This caused headlines all over the country," he said later, "and I never expected it." To keep up the attacks, McCarthy confided that he might need "some evidence." He asked friends to help him find it.

His finger-pointing grew increasingly wild and irresponsible, and many innocent people were hurt. Some Wisconsinites were so embarrassed and so upset with McCarthy that in 1954 they tried to recall him, that is, force him to run in a special election before his term was up. This attempt failed. But by then, the American public was tiring of McCarthy's antics and began to ignore his charges.

FLAG DAY

The first Flag Day was celebrated at Stony Hill School near Waubeka, Wisconsin, on June 14, 1885. The school's teacher, Bernard Cigrand, who was very patriotic, had been looking for a way to show how much he loved his country. He finally decided to establish a day to honor the flag.

Cigrand was determined to have Flag Day celebrated across the country. He repeatedly asked the government to proclaim June 14 a national holiday. Finally, in 1916, President Woodrow Wilson and Congress agreed to do so.

Today, many communities host Flag Day parades. The largest is held in Appleton, Wisconsin.

. . . PATRIOTIC

On the whole, Wisconsinites have been eager to shoulder their responsibilities as United States citizens. More than ninety thousand men from the state fought for the Union during the Civil War. Wisconsinites also served in the Spanish-American War, World War I, World War II, the Korean conflict, and Vietnam. More recently, men and women from the state served in the U.S. military in actions in Lebanon, Grenada, Panama, Kuwait (Operation Desert Storm), and peace-keeping efforts in Somalia.

That does not mean that Wisconsinites have always agreed on participating in these wars, though. During the Civil War, some German immigrants resented being drafted to fight for the Union. Many had fled their homeland in order to avoid forced military service. Similarly, many Wisconsinites of German descent opposed America's involvement in World War I, in which it fought against Germany. One of the state's two senators and nine of its eleven representatives voted against entering the war. In the early 1970s, some college students at the University of Wisconsin in Madison led demonstrations against America's involvement in the war in Vietnam. Some of these demonstrations erupted into violence.

. . . ENTHUSIASTIC SPORTS FANS

Wisconsinites might disagree about politics or whether the country should enter a war, but few argue about enjoying sports. Most people like to hunt, fish, snowmobile, cross-country ski, swim, hike, or cheer their favorite professional sports teams. These teams include the Milwaukee Bucks (basketball), the Milwaukee Brewers (baseball),

Northern Wisconsin has many cross-country ski trails and races. The biggest race, the Birkebeiner, is fifty-nine miles long and draws contestants from all over America.

and the Green Bay Packers (football). Before the Brewers, the Braves represented Milwaukee in baseball's major leagues. Led by Henry Aaron, the greatest home-run hitter in baseball history, the Braves won the World Series in 1958. When the Bucks won their only National Basketball Association championship in 1971, they were led by basketball's all-time greatest scorer, Kareem Abdul-Jabbar.

Of all the professional sports teams in the state, the Packers have been the most popular. Fans have been particularly loyal since the 1960s, when Vince Lombardi was the coach and the Packers won the first two Super Bowl games (1967 and 1968). Even though the Packers failed to return to the Super Bowl for twenty-nine years, fans still filled the stadium for every game to cheer on the team.

When the Packers finally reached the Super Bowl in 1997, fans went wild. Hundreds purchased plane tickets to New Orleans, where the game was played, just to greet the team when it arrived. Thousands went to the game. And while the Packers were pitted against the New England Patriots, the streets of Wisconsin were deserted. Everyone was glued to the television set. When the players returned victorious to Green Bay, the city held a huge welcome-back parade for the champions. Schools were closed so that children could join the celebration.

Because the "Pack" is so popular, season tickets are nearly impossible to get. Previous ticket holders are able to get tickets first. If any tickets are not claimed, fans on a waiting list may buy them. But few holders fail to buy again—even after they die! People actually include their position on the purchasing list in their wills, and their heirs are then allowed to buy tickets. So, very few who have not purchased in the past or been lucky enough to inherit from relatives can buy season tickets these days. There are now thirty thousand names on the waiting list. If the current cancellation rate continues, someone who registers today will not get tickets until the year 3001. Such fan loyalty makes the Packers a successful enterprise even though Green Bay is the National Football League's smallest city with a locally owned franchise.

It is no surprise, then, that such a popular team has produced its share of heroes. Among them is Reggie White, one of the NFL's most ferocious defensive players. Buddy Ryan, the former Philadelphia Eagles head coach, said, "Reggie White is the perfect defensive lineman . . . probably the most gifted defensive athlete I've ever been around."

But it is not just White's playing ability that makes him a hero.

White is a man who believes in helping others. He supports many charities in Green Bay, and he and his wife, Sara, have built a shelter for unwed mothers in Tennessee. White also counsels teenage gang members and abused children and gives a large portion of his income to several Baptist churches in the South. Recently, when arsonists burned down one of these churches, White led a successful drive to raise money to help the congregation rebuild. Ray Didinger, a writer for the Philadelphia *Daily News*, said that Reggie White "has touched thousands of lives. He is a man who always wore his heart on his extra-long sleeve." Wisconsin is proud to claim him as one of its own.

Reggie White was a hero in the 1997 Super Bowl. When the team returned to Green Bay after the game, Wisconsinites jammed the city's streets to catch a glimpse of the players. White said, "[A Super Bowl victory] has been a long time coming, not only for you but for me as well."

5 LEGENDS IN THEIR TIME

Women in costume at Old World Wisconsin

Wisconsinites have always been proud of their many accomplishments, especially those that make government work for the people. They are equally proud of their entertainers, writers, and clever inventors, who have given us a good laugh or moved us to think about ourselves in a new way or changed the way we get around.

PROGRESSIVE THINKERS

By the mid-nineteenth century, the United States was deeply divided over the question of slavery. Many Northerners were determined to make sure that it was not allowed to spread beyond the South. So when Congress passed a law in 1854 that would have permitted its practice in the new Kansas Territory, anti-slavery Northerners were angry. Opponents of the new law held meetings to decide how to deal with the problem.

One of these meetings took place in a small schoolhouse in Ripon, Wisconsin, on February 28. It was led by Alvan E. Bovay, a newcomer to the state who had been associated with the National Reform Association in New York. The men who attended the meeting that night decided to start a new political party to fight the spread of slavery. They called themselves Republicans. Even though a similar meeting took place in Michigan, Wisconsinites have long considered Ripon the birthplace of the Republican Party. The party's candidate for president in 1860, Abraham Lincoln, became America's sixteenth president.

Although the Republican Party in Wisconsin was very popular at first, by 1900 it was being questioned by some of its own members. Industry was booming, railroads were crisscrossing the state, and lumber companies were stripping the North Woods of every available log. Industrial leaders had become very wealthy and very powerful men. To maintain their power, they worked hand in hand with political bosses to decide who could run for office. The bosses chose candidates who they thought would pass legislation to protect the wealthy and powerful in the state.

In 1900, Robert M. La Follette decided to run for governor. After receiving the support of the Republican political bosses, La Follette focused his attention on the state's farmers and laborers. Many of these people had never received much attention from a politician before. They traveled for miles and stood for hours just to hear La Follette speak. La Follette asked his audience to "look at the record." He told them that a vote for him meant "having a government of the people" while a vote for his opponent meant "government run by public-service corporations." Wisconsinites elected him governor.

To the anger of the party bosses, La Follette and his supporters in the state legislature made sweeping changes. They even called themselves Progressive Republicans to distinguish themselves from the rest of the party. The program that they began would be followed by other Progressives for many years to come.

These politicians drafted new legislation at a dizzying speed. The bills adjusted the method of taxation so that big businesses paid their fair share, set up boards to control industry more closely, granted more funds for education, enacted child labor laws, established old-age pensions, created the first workmen's compensation program for people injured on the job, started the state park system, funded the reforestation of the North Woods, developed a statewide network of roads, and established the primary system.

The primary system, which is widely used today in state and national elections, allowed voters in Wisconsin to decide who would run for state office. Anyone who wanted to be a representative simply announced that he was a candidate. (At the time, only men could hold political office.) The candidate then presented his beliefs and programs directly to the people. The winners of each party's primary ran in the final election.

Although most Wisconsinites were pleased with the changes made by the Progressives, many of the powerful businessmen and industrialists were dismayed and even shocked by the new laws. They complained of "reform run wild."

In 1905, La Follette was elected to the U.S. Senate, where he served until his death in 1925. In the Senate, he introduced many of the programs that had been successful in Wisconsin, and a number of them were adopted nationwide. He also ran, unsuccessfully, as the Progressive Party's candidate for president of the United States in 1924.

Progressivism in Wisconsin did not die with La Follette. One son, Robert La Follette Jr., represented Wisconsin in Congress from 1925 to 1947. His other son, Phillip, served two terms as governor of the state, from 1931 to 1933 and from 1935 to 1939.

Robert La Follette was a powerful speaker. Here, he strikes his typical pose when giving a speech. No wonder he was sometimes called "Fighting Bob." He wanted, he said, "to return the government to the people."

Robert La Follette's sons, Phillip (left) and Robert Jr. (right), followed in their father's political footsteps. Phillip was elected governor of the state, and Robert Jr. became a senator.

During Phillip La Follette's time in office, Wisconsin, like the rest of the nation, was overwhelmed by economic hardships during the Great Depression. Phillip experimented with many programs to put people back to work and rebuild the economy. Wisconsin started the first unemployment compensation program in the nation.

ENTERTAINERS

In addition to having some powerful politicians, Wisconsin has been home to talented entertainers, among them actors Frederic March, Spencer Tracy, and Gene Wilder. Although all three are show-business legends, probably the state's most famous entertainer is a magician. Harry Houdini was born in 1874 and grew

One of Frederic March's most popular films was Dr. Jekyll and Mr. Hyde. Here, he is shown as both characters. Several theaters in the state are named for Mr. March.

Harry Houdini could free himself from numerous handcuffs in seconds and from locked trunks in minutes. Just before he died, Houdini promised to find a way to escape from whatever lay beyond death. On Halloween, the anniversary of his death, believers hold a séance in Appleton, in hopes that Houdini's spirit will appear. ■

up in Appleton and Milwaukee, where he began his remarkable career in a neighborhood circus. During his first performance, he hung upside down from a trapeze bar and picked up pins with his eyelids.

Years later, Houdini made his reputation by performing death-defying tricks. He was handcuffed, wrapped in chains, locked inside a trunk, and tossed into a deep river. Nervous audiences counted the seconds until he surfaced, well aware that the man had but a short time to escape from the trunk if he was to survive. Houdini never disappointed his audiences, setting a standard for escape artists and magicians that has never been matched.

Many who tried to imitate Houdini began their careers with the circus, which, since the early nineteenth century, had been especially popular in Wisconsin. Herr Dreisbach's circus, which performed in Whitewater in 1841, was the first to appear in the state. Dreisbach was followed by others, including the Mabie Brothers, who gave a show in Delavan in 1846. Wisconsin eventually became known as the Mother of Circuses because so many of them began in the state or called it home for at least part of the year. At one time twenty-three circuses wintered over in Delavan.

The best-known modern circus, the Ringling Brothers Circus, opened in Baraboo, Wisconsin, in 1884. The five Ringling brothers were Al, Charles, Alf T., Otto, and John. Their first show featured four animals—three horses and one hyena. The brothers played in the band, performed a variety of stunts, made their own costumes, and built the bleachers for their audience. With hard work, the Ringlings turned their show into a spectacle that became known as the "Greatest Show on Earth," which "performed feats of breathless wonder."

The Circus World Museum in Baraboo now houses a vast array of old Ringling wagons and circus equipment as well as many animals. In addition, the museum is home to the famous Ringling Brothers and Barnum & Bailey Clown College, which teaches students the art of being funny. Each summer, students test their skills before a live audience under the museum's big top, a tent big enough to hold two thousand spectators.

Tami Topper recently gave a performance in this tent. She dreams of becoming a legend in her time. "I hope to become a famous

Every summer, people line the railroad route used by the Great Circus Train to see the colorful wagons and the animals inside them.

clown," she said. "There are no really famous women clowns, and I could be the first."

Once a year, the Circus World Museum puts on an impressive parade for the state. The museum dusts off sixty elaborately decorated wagons, tunes up its calliope, and loads tigers and elephants onto a train of flatcars bound for Milwaukee. Thousands of spectators line the tracks to see the wagons as they pass by, and many more crowd the streets of Milwaukee to see a wonderful and unique parade.

WRITERS

Wisconsin has been the home of a number of famous writers, including Edna Ferber, Thornton Wilder, and the Pulitzer Prize-winning playwright Zona Gale. Perhaps the best known, especially among children, are Laura Ingalls Wilder and Sterling North.

Laura Ingalls Wilder (no relation to Thornton Wilder or actor Gene Wilder) was born in Pepin in a small log cabin in the woods. Many years later, she wrote about her childhood in a book called *Little House in the Big Woods*. This volume served as the first in a series. She based other books, among them *Little House on the Prairie*, *On the Banks of Plum Creek*, and *By the Shores of Silver Lake*, on her family's adventures as it moved west.

In her book Come and Get It, *Edna Ferber took to task the lumber barons who had cut down a large portion of the North Woods: "They hacked and tore and gouged and schemed and took and took and never replaced. There was no end to this richness. Thousands of miles of it, and no one to stop them."*

STERLING NORTH

Even before he found Rascal, Sterling North's life was far from typical. He was the youngest of four children whose mother had died, and he lived with his father. North had a deep love for all animals and a lot of freedom as a child, which resulted in an interesting childhood. In *Rascal*, he wrote:

> No one was concerned about the hours I kept. I was a very competent eleven-year-old. If I came home long after dark, my father would merely look up from his book to greet me vaguely and courteously. He allowed me to live my own life, keep pet skunks and woodchucks in the back yard and the barn, pamper my tame crow, my many cats, and my faithful Saint Bernard. He even let me build my eighteen-foot canoe in the living room. I had not entirely completed the framework, so it would take another year at least. When we had visitors, they sat in the easy chairs surrounding the canoe, or skirted the prow to reach the great shelves of books we were continuously lending. We lived alone and liked it, cooked and cleaned in our own fashion, and paid little attention to indignant housewives who told my father that this was no way to bring up a child.

Today, a replica of Wilder's home stands on the spot where the original house once stood. The big woods, which was cut down many years ago and turned into farmland, is being replaced one tree at a time. The trees are purchased by children in the area through a "Pennies for Laura" campaign.

Sterling North was born in 1906 and spent his boyhood near Edgerton. He hoped to become a great football player, but his career was cut short when he contracted polio, a crippling disease that made it nearly impossible for him to walk. North then turned his efforts to writing and editing. His children's book, *Rascal*, a story about his pet raccoon, is one of his most popular works.

Not all Wisconsin writers tell the truth. Some have been known to tell lies—big lies—for fame and glory. And one organization, the Burlington Liars Club, actually gives an award for the biggest whopper. This club accepts stories throughout the year. On New Year's Eve, judges meet to read the tall tales and select the winner for the year. The best lie is published in newspapers throughout the country and engraved on a plaque, which is placed on the Tall Tale Trail in Burlington.

INVENTORS

Wisconsinites invented the ice-cream sundae, a test for measuring butterfat in milk, the typewriter, and some farm machinery. Their most popular inventions, though, have been an early car and the Harley-Davidson motorcycle.

When a self-propelled automobile was driven down the streets of Racine, Wisconsin, in the early 1870s by its creator, Reverend J. W. Carhart, the car caused quite a ruckus. Horses bolted and a few women and children screamed. People stopped and stared as the auto "raced" along at four miles an hour.

News about this marvelous development traveled fast. Members of the Wisconsin legislature were so impressed that they decided to offer a reward of $10,000 to any inventor who could design something "which shall be a cheap and practical substitute for the use of horses and other animals on the highway." The invention had to be "propelled by its own internal power at the average rate of at least five miles per hour." In addition, the invention would have to prove its durability by making a two-hundred-mile trek over public roads, no easy feat in those days.

Inventors all over the state went to work to claim the prize. Shortly after, E. P. Cowles announced that he had built the winner. It was the Green Bay, which he named in honor of the city in which it was built. Frank Schomer and Anson Farriand in Oshkosh disagreed. They had their own vehicle, named after their own hometown, that they said could outdo anything else on the road.

The first auto race in the country was organized to settle the dispute. The route, now highlighted by a historical marker, ran from Green Bay to Madison. The cars left Green Bay at 11 A.M. on July 16, 1878. After numerous mechanical troubles, the contest finished on July 23, when the Oshkosh roared into Madison.

Although the legislators were impressed with the car, they were stunned by the cost to build one: $1,000. Since the lawmakers determined that this made the vehicle something less than "cheap and practical," they cut the award in half.

Other inventors in the state studied the Oshkosh carefully. They then set out to manufacture cars of their own, and by the early 1900s had produced more than fifty different kinds of automobiles. However, Wisconsin manufacturers encountered stiff competition when Henry Ford invented his assembly line in Michigan, which could mass produce cars for a very reasonable sum, and many went out of business.

Automobile inventors were not the only Wisconsinites working on motors. In 1900, Arthur Davidson, his brother Walter, and Bill

The Oshkosh, which won the first auto race in America, looked more like a tractor than a car.

Harley were also tinkering with engines. They built a special kind of motorcycle and called it the Harley-Davidson. Because these cycles required so much time to produce, initial output was very limited. In 1904, for example, the men made only two machines.

To prove that their cycles were well made, Harley and the Davidsons entered them in races. When the machines achieved a speed of twenty-five miles per hour, the public really took notice. Eventually some police departments decided to use Harley-Davidson motorcycles, and that gave the company the boost that it needed to become successful.

Today, Harley-Davidson produces about 140,000 motorcycles annually. Even though some sell for as much as $18,000, they are in great demand by cyclists. Each year, Harley owners gather at informal conventions to swap stories about their cycles. This also gives them a chance to admire other models and remember briefly the men in Wisconsin who made it all possible.

The Harley-Davidson motorcycle was well received. Today, it is one of the best-known products manufactured in Wisconsin.

6 "ESCAPE TO WISCONSIN"

Coon Creek in southwestern Wisconsin

First-time tourists in Wisconsin are often surprised by the state's changing landscape. These visitors expect to see little but thousands of acres of farmland. Although Wisconsin certainly has many beautiful farms, it also has other sights worth visiting. So, as the state's ads say, let's "Escape to Wisconsin" for a while and take in some sights, one region at a time.

THE EASTERN LOWLANDS AND RIDGES

Let's start our trip in Milwaukee, the largest city in the state. There is much here for tourists to see. The Milwaukee County Zoo, among the most highly rated zoos in the country, has over four thousand animals and birds. Brave visitors take short rides on camels or elephants. Those who prefer a more traditional means of getting around tour the grounds in a "zoomobile."

Milwaukee is also the home of the Mitchell Park Conservatory. This building has three seven-story-tall domes housing tropical, desert, and flowering plants. The tropical dome contains jungle plants, including orchids, and many birds, especially tiny finches. The desert dome has many cacti and tall palm trees. The display dome houses seasonal shows. One of the best-attended displays is the Christmas exhibit, in which thousands of red poinsettias and

Milwaukee is the state's largest city.

Christmas trees covered with tiny twinkling lights fill the dome with color and fragrance.

Milwaukee also has many forms of entertainment from which to choose. Sports fans can catch a Brewers or Bucks game, depending on the season. Music fans might attend a performance by the Milwaukee Symphony or take in a concert by a well-known celebrity at the Performing Arts Center. In addition, visitors can attend any number of festivals that are held in the city.

Restaurants and shops specialize in ethnic foods, especially German dishes, and many visitors enjoy sampling European-style cooking. Usinger's meat market sells sixty kinds of sausages, many of which are made from old German recipes.

Just southwest of Milwaukee, near Eagle, is Old World Wisconsin. This unique museum has forty structures: barns, homes, and stores that were built by some of the first immigrants to arrive in the state.

In Old World Wisconsin, costumed guides recreate village life during the mid-1800s. Old-fashioned methods are used to harvest crops and to cook food and make clothes.

These buildings were moved from their original locations to the museum's grounds. Buildings that were too large to be moved in one piece were taken apart and then reassembled when they reached Eagle.

Madison is also a popular tourist destination. The state capitol, a smaller version of the national capitol in Washington, D.C., is beautiful. It was made from marble and granite instead of wood to make sure that it would not be destroyed by fire, as an earlier structure had been in 1904. The 1917 building is topped with a high dome. Inside, the dome is decorated with an elaborate painting that shows the many resources of Wisconsin. Guides give tours (more than seventy thousand people go through the building each year), and if the legislature is holding a public debate, visitors are welcome to listen as long as they wish.

Downtown Madison is unique, an unusual blend of country and city, old and new. During the summer, farmers bring in truckloads

TEN LARGEST CITIES

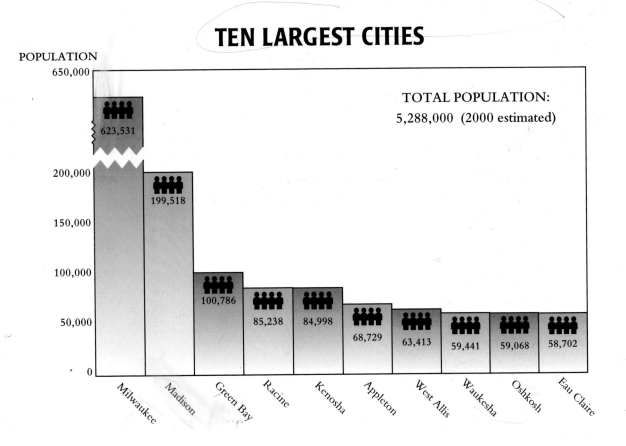

POPULATION

TOTAL POPULATION: 5,288,000 (2000 estimated)

- Milwaukee 623,531
- Madison 199,518
- Green Bay 100,786
- Racine 85,238
- Kenosha 84,998
- Appleton 68,729
- West Allis 63,413
- Waukesha 59,441
- Oshkosh 59,068
- Eau Claire 58,702

The Madison Farmer's Market has more than one hundred fifty vendors. Buyers come early in the day to get the best of the just-picked strawberries, or bread still warm from the oven.

of tomatoes, melons, and sweet corn to sell on the capitol's sidewalks. Opposite this rural scene are some of the trendiest art shops and clothing stores in the state. Nearby, the Wisconsin State Historical Society gathers information from the past, while just down the street, forty thousand University of Wisconsin students prepare for the future.

About eighty miles northeast of Madison is Oshkosh. Oshkosh is the home of the Experimental Aircraft Association, which draws thousands of people from all over the world to its annual Fly-In each summer. While the Fly-In is in session, the Oshkosh airport is the busiest in the world. Owners of experimental airplanes meet to share their love of flying and to learn new techniques for building better planes. Aircraft used in World Wars I and II as well as huge jets, such as the Concorde, appear in special programs, as do dare-devil stunt pilots. Throughout the year, visitors can watch films about experimental aircraft in the museum's auditorium and look at numerous planes and aviation displays in several buildings.

All of Door County, the thumblike peninsula that juts out into Lake Michigan, is a tourist destination. In spring, seven thousand acres of flowering cherry trees and one million daffodil bulbs put on a colorful show. In summer, tourists visit lighthouses, relax on sandy beaches, catch big fish in Lake Michigan, and hike the many trails in four state parks. The county is also home to many artists, and visitors can watch potters and painters at work and buy original works of art in local galleries.

In addition, Door County restaurants offer some tasty treats. Almost every eatery has some kind of cherry dessert: pies, cobblers, or crisps, which are topped with rich vanilla ice cream. When

PLACES TO SEE

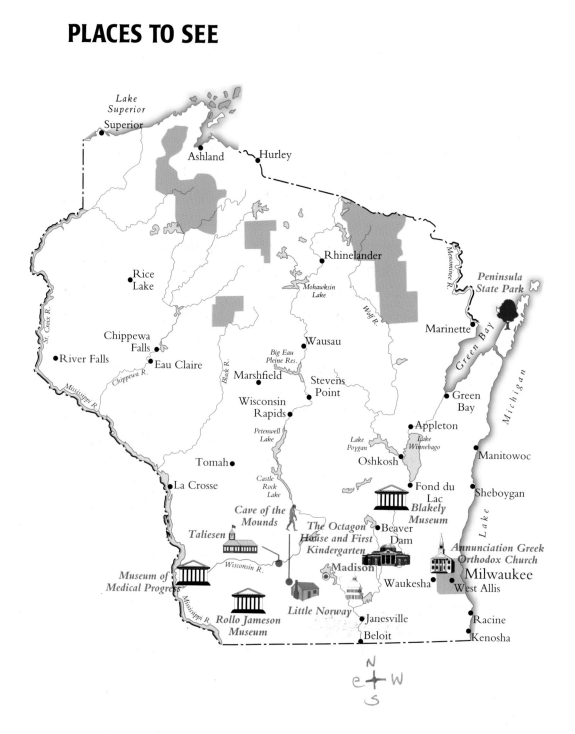

Lake
Superior

Superior

Ashland • Hurley

Rice
Lake

Rhinelander

Mohawksin
Lake

St. Croix R.

Peninsula
State Park

Menominee R.

Wolf R.

Marinette

Chippewa
Falls

River Falls

Eau Claire

Chippewa R.

Black R.

Wausau

Big Eau
Pleine Res.

Marshfield

Green
Bay

Green Bay

Michigan

Wisconsin
Rapids

Stevens
Point

Mississippi R.

Petenwell
Lake

Tomah

Castle
Rock
Lake

Lake
Poygan

Lake
Winnebago

Appleton

Oshkosh

Manitowoc

La Crosse

Cave of the
Mounds

Taliesen

Wisconsin R.

The Octagon
House and First
Kindergarten

Beaver
Dam

Fond du
Lac

Blakely
Museum

Sheboygan

Lake

Museum of
Medical Progress

Rollo Jameson
Museum

Madison

Little Norway

Mississippi R.

Annunciation Greek
Orthodox Church

Milwaukee

Waukesha

West Allis

Janesville

Beloit

Racine

Kenosha

N
e + W
S

visitors want something more substantial than dessert, they head to restaurants that serve fresh fish cooked over a wood fire.

THE NORTH WOODS

One of the best-known towns in the North Woods is Peshtigo. By 1871, most of the nearby area had been logged off, and acres of old stumps and piles of pine needles baked dry by a summer drought surrounded much of the village. So, on October 8, 1871, when a local fire got out of hand, the blaze spread rapidly. Fanned by high winds, the flames roared through the village so quickly that eight hundred residents were killed within minutes. The roaring fire continued on its path of destruction, burning a swath forty miles long and ten miles wide in only four hours. In all, 1,200 people were killed. The Peshtigo Fire Museum tells the dramatic story of America's greatest fire disaster.

Hayward is another North Woods community with an interesting history. Like Peshtigo, this town was once surrounded by logging camps. The men who lived there worked from dawn to dusk. The work was so strenuous that few of them remained loggers for more than a couple of years. To pass the long nights away from friends and families, they sang scandalous songs and made up tall tales about life as a lumberjack. Hayward's attractions include shows about what it was like to be a lumberjack long ago.

Equally popular are the many crystal-clear lakes in the area. The bottoms and shores are covered by a sand so fine that it is called sugar sand. Families often rent cottages here for a week or two to swim and fish. When the fish are not biting, disappointed anglers

Hayward hosts the Lumberjack World Championships in the summer. Participants show off their skills by cutting a tree into pieces at lightning speed, racing up tall poles, and maintaining their balance on spinning logs.

visit the National Freshwater Fishing Hall of Fame in Hayward. The four-story museum is shaped like a giant muskie.

Hayward is also a popular winter spot for visitors who like to snowmobile or ski. The Birkebeiner, the largest cross-country ski race in the country, is held near Hayward. More than six thousand participants enter this race every year.

North of Hayward is Pattison State Park, where Big Manitou Falls is located. At 165 feet, Big Manitou is the highest of the area's many waterfalls.

THE HORRIBLE HODAG

One of the most entertaining of Wisconsin's tall tales comes from the North Woods. It is the tale of the hodag, which Gene Shepard, a prankster, supposedly stumbled upon in 1896 in the woods near Rhinelander. This animal, according to Shepard, breathed fire, just as dragons did long ago, and posed in a very menacing fashion. The creature, he told everyone who would listen, was mean, *really* mean.

To capture the hodag, Shepard enlisted the help of friends who were known to wrestle bears for fun. The men tiptoed to the hodag's den and stuck a long pole topped with a chloroform-saturated rag into the cave. The strange creature was overcome by the chloroform and passed out. As soon as it was safe to do so, the men rushed in, bound the hodag, and took it to Shepard's place.

Word spread about the hodag. To accommodate everyone who wanted to see it, Shepard took his discovery to county fairs, where he allowed a few people at a time to enter his dimly lit tent for a quick peek. People were awestruck by the alligatorlike critter, which had two horns on its head and twelve spikes down its back. Some spectators were even frightened when the animal began to move toward them.

Eventually, everyone heard about the hodag, thanks to articles that appeared in many newspapers. When word reached the Smithsonian Institution in Washington, D.C., scientists there announced that they were heading to Rhinelander to study the animal. Shepard then had to admit that the whole thing was a joke. The hodag that people had seen was made of wooden parts that moved when Shepard pulled the right wires.

Today, a statue of a hodag stands on the outskirts of Rhinelander. It is the mascot of the city and a reminder of one of Shepard's most successful pranks.

Bayfield, on the shore of Lake Superior, is the gateway to the Apostle Islands, the northernmost point in the state. Tourists catch ferries here to visit the twenty-two islands, including Madeline Island, the only one of the Apostles with year-round residents. These people are thought to be some of the hardiest in the state. When ferry service stops in late fall, the islanders are isolated until the lake freezes solid between Madeline and Bayfield. They can then drive their snowmobiles or cars over the ice to the shore.

The beautiful Apostle Islands have been designated as a national lakeshore. The redness of the rock, caused by iron in the stone, against the bright blue waters of the world's largest freshwater lake makes a colorful scene.

The National Freshwater Fishing Hall of Fame is not a typical museum.

In summer, waves from Lake Superior splash against the soft sandstone cliffs of Wisconsin's north shore, forming caves. In the winter, some of the lake's water freezes when it hits the rocks, creating dramatic ice caves.

The fishing in this area is great. Lake trout, perch, and pike are abundant. Commercial guides take fishermen to the best spots, making it nearly impossible for any angler to end the day empty-handed.

THE CENTRAL PLAIN

The wetlands, sometimes called the "Great Swamp of Wisconsin," dominate the Central Plain. Here wildlife thrives in a national preserve as well as in state refuges. The Sandhill Wildlife Demonstration Area is a temporary home for at least five thousand sandhill cranes in October, when the birds seek a safe resting site on their annual southward migration.

Nearby, cranberries are raised in huge bogs. When the fruit is ready for picking, tour buses arrive with visitors eager to attend local cranberry festivals and watch workers harvest the fruit. By this time, the berries are floating on top of water that was forced into the bogs to separate the berries from their plants. Workers "rake" the berries together and put them into containers. Once the fruit is cleaned and packaged, it is sent all over the country.

On the southern edge of the Central Plain lies the Wisconsin Dells. According to Indian legend, the Dells' seven-mile-long canyon was carved out by a huge serpent that moved southward through the area. In reality, water from the last glacier began to shape this site about twelve thousand years ago. When the glacier thawed, some of the meltwater was dammed up behind rocks, creating a huge lake. Eventually, the water broke through the dam and rushed southward, sculpting a new riverbed and the Dells. Over the years, water, wind, and frost sculpted the soft sandstone into strange formations. These shapes have been given descriptive names such as the Beehive and the Grand Piano.

Most visitors tour the area, which is divided into the Upper and Lower Dells, on flat-bottomed boats called "ducks." Others take in the sights by strolling along boardwalks that meander through places

The Wisconsin Dells has long been regarded as a sacred site by Native Americans.

such as Cold Water Canyon, a good place to be on a hot summer day.

Northwest of the Dells, Mill Bluff State Park contains more unusual rock formations. The pillarlike shapes were once islands in the glacial lake. Water wore away the softest stone over thousands of years. Today, visitors can only imagine what the islands looked like thousands of years ago.

Mill Bluff is now part of the Ice Age National Scientific Reserve. The reserve has nine sections that outline the edge of the last glacier. Currently, Wisconsin is purchasing land and developing a hiking trail that will connect these sections. The final trail will be more than one thousand miles long, enabling hikers to see first-hand the effects that the glacier had on the state.

THE WESTERN UPLANDS

The last region, the Western Uplands, is edged on the west by the St. Croix and Mississippi Rivers. Scattered along the waterways, especially the Mississippi, are many small towns. Most were built in tiers on the steep bluffs that face the river. Some of the oldest buildings, former banks, feed mills, and bars, have been restored. They now serve as art shops and quaint restaurants.

Most visitors tour the area by following the Old River Road, Highway 35. Others take paddle-wheel boat tours on the Mississippi or rent a houseboat and spend a week or two on the river.

Small villages in the center of the region are full of surprises. An old flour mill in Augusta reminds visitors more of New England than of Wisconsin. The Norske Nook, a small café in Osseo, serves the most famous pies in the state. Many cheese factories in the southern part of the Uplands sell cheddar, Colby, Swiss, and Limburger, as well as cheese curds freshly made each day.

Two of the best-known homes in the state, Taliesen and the House on the Rock, are located near Spring Green. Taliesen was once the home of Frank Lloyd Wright, a world-famous architect from Wisconsin. Wright believed that buildings should blend into their surroundings. Therefore, many of his designs, like Taliesen, were no taller than the surrounding foliage, and most were made from local stone and wood.

The House on the Rock was built by Alex Jordon. This house,

according to local rumors, was built to outdo Wright's Taliesen. Jordon's house is set partially on top of a large sandstone rock and partially in the rock itself. Large portions of the walls are carved out of the stone, as are the stairs and some of the benches and tables. But spectacular as it is, the house is not the main attraction. Beneath the house is a maze of rooms filled with an incredible variety of items, including clocks from Germany, ships in bottles, old dentistry tools, antique cash registers, whole storefronts that were typical of Main Street shops years ago, and a gigantic merry-go-round. In short, the House on the Rock has something for everyone—a lot like Wisconsin itself.

House on the Rock is a popular tourist destination. It has fourteen buildings, each of which holds special collections.

THE FLAG: *The state seal appears in the center of the flag. The word "Wisconsin" is at the top of the flag. The year Wisconsin became a state, 1848, appears under the shield. The flag was adopted in 1913.*

THE SEAL: *A sailor and a miner support a shield with symbols for agriculture, mining, shipping, and manufacturing. Wisconsin's loyalty to the Union is symbolized by a small United States coat of arms. A badger sits above the shield and represents the state's nickname, the Badger State. The state seal was adopted in 1881.*

STATE SURVEY

Statehood: May 29, 1848

Origin of Name: An Indian word, which may have several possible meanings including *gathering of the waters*

Nickname: The Badger State

Capital: Madison

Motto: Forward

Bird: Robin

Animal: Badger

Fish: Muskellunge

Insect: Honeybee

Flower: Wood violet

Tree: Sugar maple

Rock: Red granite

Fossil: Trilobite

Mineral: Galena

Badger

Wood violet

ON, WISCONSIN!

The music for "On, Wisconsin!" was composed in 1909 and entered in a Minnesota contest for the creation of a new football song. Instead, the composer was persuaded to dedicate it to the University of Wisconsin football team. In 1913, lyrics better suited to a state song were added. Although "On, Wisconsin!" was recognized as Wisconsin's song for many years, the state did not officially adopt it until 1959.

Words by
J. S. Hubbard and C.D. Rosa

Music by William T. Purdy

GEOGRAPHY

Highest Point: 1,952 feet above sea level, at Timms Hill

Lowest Point: 581 feet above sea level, along shore of Lake Michigan

Area: 56,153 square miles

Greatest Distance, North to South: 314 miles

Greatest Distance, East to West: 293 miles

Bordering States: Upper peninsula of Michigan to the north, Illinois to the south, Iowa and Minnesota to the west

Hottest Recorded Temperature: 114° F, at Wisconsin Dells, July 13, 1936

Coldest Recorded Temperature: −54° F, at Danbury, January 24, 1922

Average Annual Precipitation: 20 inches

Major Rivers: Bad, Chippewa, Fox, Iron, La Crosse, Manitowoa, Menominee, Milwaukee, Mississippi, Montreal, Oconto, Rock, Saint Croix, Sheboygan, Wisconsin, Wolf

Major Lakes: Big Green, Geneva, Mendota, Monoma, Pepin, Poygan, Winnebago

Trees: aspen, beech, birch, hemlock, hickory, maple, oak, red pine, spruce, white pine

Wild Plants: black currant, blueberry, fern, huckleberry, Juneberry

Animals: bear, beaver, coyote, deer, fox, gray wolf, raccoon, skunk, woodchuck

Trumpeter swan

Birds: chickadee, coot, duck, goose, grouse, jacksnipe, loon, partridge, pheasant, quail, robin, swallow, warbler, wren

Fish: bass, muskellunge, pike, sturgeon, trout

Endangered Animals: barn owl, Blanchard's cricket frog, Canada lynx, ornate box turtle, peregrine falcon, skipjack herring, slender glass lizard, timber wolf, trumpeter swan, yellow-throated warbler

Endangered Plants: brook grass, Carolina anemone, chestnut sedge, mountain cranberry, Lake Huron tansy, pine-drop, rough white lettuce, sand violet, spotted pondweed, wild petunia

TIMELINE

Wisconsin History

A.D. **700** Mound builders construct effigies in the area

800–1600 The Winnebago, Ottawa, Sioux, and Chippewa arrive in Wisconsin

1634 Jean Nicolet, the first known white man, reaches Green Bay

1673 Father Marquette and Louis Jolliet arrive in Wisconsin

1763 Wisconsin becomes part of British territory

1783 Colonies gain independence from Britain; Wisconsin is now part of the United States

1848 Wisconsin becomes the thirtieth state

1851 First state fair is held

1851 The first railroad, which runs from Milwaukee to Waukesha, begins service

1854 The Republican Party is founded in Ripon

1861–1865 About 90,000 Wisconsinites fight for the Union during the Civil War

1868 Christopher Latham Sholes patents the first typewriter

1871 Peshtigo fire kills 1,200 people

1884 Ringling Brothers Circus starts in Baraboo

1890 Dr. Stephen Babcock develops a test to measure butterfat content of milk

1900 Robert M. La Follette is elected governor, the first governor to have been born in the state

1900 Population of state reaches 2 million

1917 Present capitol completed in Madison

1931 Wisconsin enacts nation's first state unemployment compensation law

1946 Joseph McCarthy is elected to U.S. Senate

1967–1968 Green Bay Packers win first two Super Bowls

1970 Earth Day is founded by Wisconsin Senator Gaylord Nelson

1972 Milwaukee Brewers baseball team is founded

1982 Milwaukee Brewers win the World Series

1996 Shirley Abrahamson becomes first woman to hold office of chief justice of the Wisconsin Supreme Court

1997 Green Bay Packers win Super Bowl

ECONOMY

Agricultural Products: apples, barley, cranberries, dairy products, green peas, livestock, oats, potatoes, snap peas, soybeans, sweet corn, wheat

Manufactured Products: automobiles, electrical equipment, machinery, medical supplies, paper products, plumbing fixtures, process foods

Natural Resources: basalt, clay, gravel, iron, lead, quartzite, rich soil, sand, sandstone, zinc

Business and Trade: finance, insurance, real estate, retail, tourism

CALENDAR OF CELEBRATIONS

Northern Exposure/Wolf River Rendezvous In January, you can enjoy the brisk air of winter while watching top sled dog racers from Europe, Canada, and the United States compete in this three-day event in Shawano.

Championship Snowmobile Derby More than 300 professional snowmobile racers from all over the world compete for the world championship and other prizes at Eagle River in mid-January.

Hot Air Affair Over 40 hot air balloons compete in this race held every February over the St. Croix River Valley near Hudson. Watch a torchlight parade during which the balloon pilots and crews light up the darkness with fire from their balloon baskets.

Snowflake International Ski Jump Tournament Westby, the U.S. home of ski jumping, hosts world-class jumpers during this February contest. The five ski jumps in Westby are used to train Olympic ski hopefuls.

Sons of Norway Barnebirkie Birkebeiner hosts America's largest cross-country ski event for children in February. More than 1,700 children participate, ranging in age from 3 to 13.

Door County Festival of Blossoms Enjoy a magnificent view of more than one million daffodils, wildflowers, and tulips in early May. Visitors can also enjoy boat tours of several lighthouses.

Syttende Mai In May, Stoughton honors its Norwegian heritage with the longest-running Norwegian Independence Day festival held outside of Norway. There's plenty to do, including parades, folk dancing, an ugly troll contest, and arts and crafts.

Inland Sea Symposium Red Cliff Chippewa Reservation celebrates nature and its valuable resources with this June event. You can learn about camping or ecosystems or join one of 12 paddle excursions.

Summerfest If you like music, be sure to stop in Milwaukee for this 11-day festival that runs from late June to early July. You can hear your favorite music, watch professional athletes give demonstrations, and have your face painted before going to one of the circus shows.

The One and Only Great Circus Parade Week Circus wagons arrive in Milwaukee from Baraboo on July 9 for three days of performances under the big top.

NFL Training Camps/"The Cheese League" Football fans get a treat in July when several NFL teams delight spectators with scrimmages and exhibition games at "Cheese League" towns: Platteville, La Crosse, River Falls, and Green Bay.

German Fest The Milwaukee Symphony Orchestra livens up the city with an oompah band and classical music in July. This is the largest German festival of its kind, and it offers tuba playing contests, fireworks, and plenty of German food.

Lumberjack World Championship Even though this is a professional contest, amateurs can enjoy the fun at this Hayward contest held every July. Kids can enter log rolling events, and adults can chop and saw their way to prizes.

Experimental Aircraft Association International Fly-In The world's largest aviation event takes place every July and August in Oshkosh at Wittman Regional Airport. More than 11,000 airplanes—all sizes, shapes, and types—come from around the world. You can learn the history and mechanics of flight.

Indian Summer in Milwaukee Native American tribes from around the country participate in this September festival. Singing, dancing, drumming, colorful costumes, and basket weaving are some of the highlights.

Watermelon Seed-Spitting & Speed-Eating Championship Bring an appetite to Pardeeville so you can participate in this national competition. Can you beat the current record: 2.5 pounds of watermelon in 3.5 seconds? Maybe you can find out next September.

Laura Ingalls Wilder Festival Travel back in time to the mid-1800s as you visit Pepin for this September event. See performances of the stories and songs from the *Little House* books. You can visit blacksmiths, ironworkers, and weavers who are dressed in period costume.

Oktoberfest La Crosse hosts this annual celebration in September and October. Taste ethnic food, take a carnival ride, and listen to German music.

Display of 6,000 Santas From November to January, you can see the amazing collection of life-size santas at House on the Rock in Spring Green. The house is decorated for the holidays, which makes this a perfect way to get into the spirit of Christmas.

STATE STARS

Shirley Abrahamson (1933–   ), a lawyer, was the first woman to be appointed and elected to the Wisconsin Supreme Court.

Stephen Moulton Babcock (1843–1931) taught at the University of Wisconsin. He was a chemist who developed the test that determines the amount of butterfat in dairy products.

John Bardeen (1908–1991) was born in Madison. He earned many distinguished awards during his 60-year career and was still publishing scientific papers at the age of 83. He shared the Nobel Prize in physics in 1956 with W. H. Brattain and W. Shockley for research leading to the invention of the transistor. In 1972, he shared the Nobel Prize with L. N. Cooper and J. R. Schrieffer for the theory of superconductivity.

John Bardeen

Ada Deer (1935–   ) won national recognition for her work to restore the Menominee Indians to reservation status. She was born on the Menominee Indian Reservation in Wisconsin and taught Native American Studies at the University of Wisconsin in Madison.

Ada Deer

Edna Ferber (1885–1968) began her writing career at age 17 as a newspaper reporter in Appleton. Her novels and plays offer an accurate portrayal of American life in the 1920s and 1930s. Her novel *So Big* won the Pulitzer Prize in 1925, and *Show Boat* became a popular musical stage play. Ferber was hailed as the greatest woman novelist of her time.

Zona Gale (1874–1938) was born in Portage. She used her writing to support feminism and racial equality. The play based on her novel *Miss Lulu Bett* won the 1921 Pulitzer Prize in drama, which made Gale the first woman to win the prize.

Cordelia Harvey (1824–1895) was called the "Wisconsin Angel" because she made many visits to hospitalized Civil War soldiers.

Woodrow Charles (Woody) Herman (1913–1987) was a famous jazz musician and bandleader who was born in Milwaukee. He founded a band, Woody Herman and His Orchestra, which played a style of music that excited both musicians and non-musicians. Herman and his band were very successful with this blend of music that Herman believed was true jazz.

Harry Houdini (1874–1926) grew up in Appleton. Born Erich Weiss in Hungary, he was one of the most famous escape artists.

Vince Lombardi (1913–1970) coached the Green Bay Packers from 1959 to 1968. The Packers won five league titles and two Super Bowl championships under this beloved coach's leadership.

Joseph Raymond McCarthy (1908–1957) was born in Grand Chute. As a Republican U.S. senator, he led a harsh crusade against individuals whom he believed to support the Communist Party. Eventually, he was censured by the U.S. Senate for misconduct.

Golda Meir (1893–1978) was born in Kiev, Russia, but grew up in Milwaukee. In 1921, she emigrated to Palestine, which is now Israel, where she became a great leader. She served as foreign minister from 1956 to 1965. During this time, she worked with cooperative planning programs between Israel and Africa. In 1969, the Labor Party nominated Golda Meir to be prime minister, a position she held until she retired from political life in 1974. She is still recognized and respected for her dedication to her country and concern for people.

Golda Meir

William L. (Billy) Mitchell (1879–1936) learned to fly from Orville Wright. Although he commanded air forces in World War I, he was demoted because he criticized military officials. By 1942, he was serving alongside other officers as a major general.

John Muir (1838–1914) was an explorer and naturalist who was born in Marquette County. Muir loved nature and saw beauty in the smallest wonders of the natural world. He had little formal schooling but was always learning new things and developing new interests. His first wilderness adventure was a 1,000-mile walk from Louisville, Kentucky, to Savannah, Georgia. Love of nature and concern for its preservation led to his founding, with Robert Underwood Johnson, of The Sierra Club.

Georgia O'Keeffe (1887–1986) is well known for her paintings of nature. She was born in Sun Prairie but moved to west Texas as a young adult, where she first taught art in the Amarillo public schools and later at West Texas State University. The desert landscape of the Southwest inspired her; its influence is seen in her many paintings. She married photographer Alfred Stieglitz and eventually settled near Taos, New Mexico, in 1949.

Georgia O'Keeffe

William Hubbs Rehnquist (1924–), born in Milwaukee, was appointed chief justice of the U. S. Supreme Court in 1986 by President Reagan. He is against the death penalty and believes it is constitutional to exclude women from the draft.

William Hubbs Rehnquist

Ringling Brothers Albert (1852–1916), Otto (1858–1911), Alfred T. (1861–1919), Charles (1863–1926), John (1866–1936) operated a touring circus before establishing the Ringling Brothers Circus in 1884. When the brothers bought the Barnum and Bailey Circus in 1907, theirs became the leading circus in the country. They were born in Baraboo.

Margarethe Schurz (1833–1876) was a teacher who opened the first U. S. kindergarten in Watertown in 1856.

(George) Orson Welles (1915–1985) was born in Kenosha. An actor and director known for his influential artistic independence, he earned a reputation as a director while in his early twenties. His first film, *Citizen Kane*, was based on publisher William Randolph Hearst. *Citizen Kane* is ranked as one of the most important films in motion picture history; it is highly regarded for its camera and sound techniques. Welles's radio drama, *The War of the Worlds*, realistically portrayed a Martian invasion.

Orson Welles

Frank Lloyd Wright (1867–1959) was one of this country's most influential architects. He built his own home, which he called Taliesen, in Spring Green, Wisconsin. His style was known as "organic architecture" because the buildings were styled so that they reflected their natural surroundings. One of the buildings he designed was the Imperial Hotel in Tokyo.

TOUR THE STATE

The Logging Museum (Rhinelander) This logging camp reproduction features a bunkhouse, a blacksmith's house, a sawmill, and displays of logging equipment.

Circle M Corral (Minocqua) This amusement park has go-carts, bumper boats, horseback riding, video games, and miniature golf.

Aqualand Wildlife Park (Boulder Junction) This natural reserve has a petting zoo for children, and visitors can see most varieties of Wisconsin's wildlife in this park.

Green Bay Packer Hall of Fame (Green Bay) Here you can view the history of one of the NFL's most successful teams. See the trophy from their first Super Bowl victory and other mementos from the Packers' early days. Pictures, uniforms, equipment, and hands-on exhibits highlight the displays.

National Railroad Museum (Green Bay) See exhibits from the steam and diesel eras, General Eisenhower's staff train, and a "Big Boy" steam locomotive.

Oshkosh B'Gosh, Inc. (Oshkosh) Take a free tour of the factory where some of America's best-known children's clothes are made.

Indian Mound Park (Sheboygan) The mounds are believed to have been built between A.D. 700 and 1000. By walking the hiking trail, you can see a dozen burial grounds.

Milwaukee Art Museum (Milwaukee) The museum's collection features European and American art of the nineteenth and twentieth centuries. You can see works by Degas, Piccasso, Georgia O'Keeffe, and Andy Warhol.

Milwaukee County Historical Center (Milwaukee) The museum presents a historically accurate doctor's office and an old-fashioned drugstore. Photographs show how Milwaukee has grown in the last century.

Milwaukee Public Museum (Milwaukee) This building houses the fourth largest collection of natural history exhibits in the United States. You can also walk through a rain forest exhibit and visit dinosaurs.

Allen-Bradley Company Clock (Milwaukee) This landmark is in the *Guiness Book of World Records* as "the largest four-faced clock in the world." Ships sometimes use the clock as a reference point.

Bodamer Log Cabin Museum (Milwaukee) A wonderful example of log cabins built in the 1830s. After layers of plaster, laths, and siding were removed, the logs were found to be in great condition.

Famous Amos Cookie Studio (Milwaukee) Enjoy the Hawaiian decor and kazoo music as you munch on delicious cookies. Fun for all.

Henry Villas Park Zoo (Madison) Although this is a fun trip any time of year, you can ride a camel during the summer months, and all year round you can pet and feed the animals at the children's zoo. This is one of the city's most popular family attractions.

Circus World Museum (Baraboo) Here you can see displays of circus equipment from all over the country. You can also view some of the items used by the Ringling Brothers when they started their circus in 1884.

Myrick Park Zoo (La Crosse) Here you'll find a small collection of domestic and wild animals. Visitors can enjoy picnic areas, a wading pool, and a nature trail.

Paul Bunyan Logging Camp (Eau Claire) Visitors are greeted by a statue of the fictional lumberjack and his faithful ox, Babe, at the entrance. The museum has exhibits such as a cook shanty, a bunkhouse, and a blacksmith's shop.

FUN FACTS

Wisconsin is not called the Badger State because a large number of these cute animals live in the state. Instead, the state earned its nickname because lead miners lived in dugouts like badgers.

The first kindergarten in the United States opened in 1856 in Watertown.

William Horlick invented malted milk in 1887 in Racine.

FIND OUT MORE

BOOKS

For more information about Wisconsin, its history, and its people, check out the following books from your school or public library:

Cook, Diana. *Wisconsin Capitol: Fascinating Facts.* Madison, Wisc.: Prairie Oak Press, 1991.

Fradin, Dennis Brindell. *From Sea to Shining Sea: Wisconsin.* Chicago: Childrens Press, 1993.

Henderson, Margaret, Ethel Speerschneider, and Helen L. Ferslev. *It Happened Here: Stories of Wisconsin.* Madison: State Historical Society of Wisconsin, 1949.

Krull, Kathleen. *One Nation, Many Tribes: How Kids Live in Milwaukee's Indian Community.* New York: Lodestar/Dutton, 1995.

Stein, R. Conrad. *America the Beautiful: Wisconsin.* Chicago: Childrens Press, 1987.

To learn more about famous people from Wisconsin, read:

Greene, Carol. *John Muir: Man of Wild Places.* Chicago: Childrens Press, 1991.

———. *Laura Ingalls Wilder: Author of the Little House Books*. Chicago: Childrens Press, 1990.

Lorbiecki, Marybeth. *Of Things Natural, Wild, and Free: A Story about Aldo Leopold*. Minneapolis: Carolrhoda Books, Inc., 1993.

Rubin, Susan. *Frank Lloyd Wright*. New York: Abrams, 1994.

Thorne-Thomsen, Kathleen. *Frank Lloyd Wright for Kids*. Chicago: Review Press, 1994.

The following stories tell what it was like to be a child growing up in Wisconsin:

Brink, Carol Ryrie. *Caddie Woodlawn*. New York: Aladdin Books, 1990 (© 1935).

North, Sterling. *Rascal*. New York: Puffin, 1990 (© 1963).

Wilder, Laura Ingalls. *Little House in the Big Woods*. New York: Harper-Collins, 1990 (© 1932).

VIDEOTAPES

These videotapes will take you to some of the most popular spots in the state:

"Wisconsin's Great River Road." St. Germain, Wisc.: Discovery Productions, 1994.

"Wisconsin Dells." St. Germain, Wisc.: Discovery Productions, 1993.

"Old World Wisconsin." St. Germain. Wisc.: Discovery Productions, 1991.

INTERNET

On the Internet, you can find the State of Wisconsin Home Page, which will have pictures, facts, and suggestions for further research about the state. Go to www.state.wi.us on the World Wide Web.

INDEX

Page numbers for illustrations are in boldface.

Aaron, Henry, 85
Abdul-Jabbar, Kareem, 85
Abrahamson, Shirley, 56,
    131
actors, 94, **94**
African Americans, 74, 75
Allouez, Claude-Jean, 36
Amish (people), 57, **58**
animals, 8, 16, 18, 26, 27,
    27, 32, 34, 106, 125,
    126
Apostle Islands, 116
Appleton, 83, 95, 109
architecture, **51**, **52**, 108-
    109, 120-121
arts and crafts, **31**, 111
    cave art, 30-31
    Christmas, 106-107,
        131
    needlework, 76-77
    quillwork, **34**
    rosemaling, 80
Asians (Hmongs), 74, 75,
    76-77, **78**
Augusta, 120
aviation, 111, 130
Aztalans (Indians), 31-32

Baraboo, 96
Bayfield, 116
Bazzell, Darrell, 62
Becker, Chris, 69
birds, 8, 18, **18**, 26, 106,
    118, 126
Black Hawk (Indian), 43
Bovay, Alvan E., 90
Burlington, 100

car, 100-102, **101**
Carhart, J. W., 100
Catlin, George, **33**
celebrations, 34, 68, **68**,
    75, 76, **76**, 77, **78**,
    79, 80, 83, 86, 97,
    97, 107, **114**, 118,
    128-131
Chippewa Indians, 34, **34**,
    61-62
Cigrand, Bernard, 83
circus, 95, 96, 97, **97**, 130,
    135, 137
climate, 21-23, **23**, 125
Coon Creek, **104**
Cowles, E. P., 101
crime rate, 60

dairy industry, 47, 63, 64,
    65, **65**, **66**, 120
death penalty, 60-61
Delavan, 96
Deming, Edwin W., Indi-
    ans, **35**
Didinger, Ray, 87
disasters, 113
Dodge, Henry, **42**, 42-43
Door County, 47, 111,
    113
Dreisbach, Herr, 96

Eagle, 107, 108
Eau Claire, 109
economy, 47, 62-66, 68-
    71, 94, 128
education, 56-57, **58**, 59-
    60, 92

endangered species, 26,
    27, **27**, 126
environmental protection,
    14, 16, 26
equal rights, 61-62
ethnic groups, 54, 74, 75
exploration, 32, 36

farming, **45**, 47, 62, 63-66,
    65, 68-69, 128
    products, 64, 65-66,
        66, 68, 109, **110**,
        111, 118
Farriand, Anson, 101
Ferber, Edna, 9, 98, **98**,
    132
fish, 16, 26, 126
Fish Creek, 75
food, 111, 120
    celebrations, 77, 81,
        131
    ethnic, 107
    recipe, 67
forests, 24-25, 25, **25**
Fromader, George Adam,
    44
fur trade, 32, 36, 37-38, 39

Gayle, Zona, 98, 132
geography, 16, 18, 19
ginseng, 66, 68
government, 54-56, 62
    politics, 81-82, 90-92,
        94
Green Bay, 20, 36, 86, 87,
    101, 102, 109
Griffith, E. M., 24

Harley-Davidson motorcycle, 100, 102-103, **103**
Hastings, Bob, 71
hats, 69, **70**
Hayward, 113, 114, **114**
Hispanics, 74, 75
history, 38-39, 40, 41, 126-128
Houdini, Harry, 94-96, **95**, 133

jobs, 44, 62-66, 68-70, 92, 94
Jolliet, Louis, 36, **37**
Jordan, Alex, 120

Kenosha, 20, 109

La Follette, Phillip, 92, **93**, 94
La Follette, Robert Jr., 92, **93**
La Follette, Robert M., 91, 92, **93**
Ladoga, 47
Lake Michigan, 13, **13**, 14
Lake Superior, 13, 14, **117**
Lake Winnebago, 14, 125
lakes, 13, **13**, 14, 113, 116, **117**, 125
Lasee, Alan, 61
Leopold, Aldo, 8, 26
Liars Club, 100, 115
logging songs, 48-49, 113
Lombardi, Vince, 9, 85, 133
Lysne, Per, 80

Mabie Brothers, 96
Madeline Island, 116
Madison, 20, 31, 41, **52-53**, 84, 102, 108, 109, **110**, 111
magic, 94-96
manufacturing, 62, 69, 128
maps, 2, 15, 64, 112
Marathon County, 66
March, Frederic, 94, **94**

Marquette, Father Jacques, 36, 37, **37**
marshlands (wetlands), 14, 16, **18**, 118
McCarthy, Joseph, 81, 82, **82**, 133
Menominee Indians, **33**
Milwaukee, 20, 40, 47, 68, 75, 84, 85, 97, 106-107, **107**, 109
mining, 39, **39**, 40
mound builders, 30, 31, 32, 126, 136
Muir, John, 8, 23-24, 134
museums, 31, 38, **88**, 96, 97, 107-108, **108**, 111, 114, **116**, 136-138
music, 107, 129, 130

Native Americans, 19, 30, 31, 32, **33**, 34, **34**, 35, **35**, 36, 37, 38, **38**, 39, 40, 41, 43, 61-62, 74, 75, 77, **78**, 126
Nelson, Gaylord, 81
New Glarus, **79**
nickname, 40, 123
Nicolet, Jean, 32, 35, **35**, 36, 126
North, Sterling, 98, 99-100
North Woods, 16, **17**, 24, 47, 113-117

Oshkosh, 77, 101, 109, 111, 136
Osseo, 120

parks, 31, 32, 36, 70, 92, 111, 114, 119
patriotism, 83, 84
people, famous, 131-135
    entertainers, 94-97
    inventors, 100-103
    politics, 81-82, 90-94
    writers, 98-100
Peshtigo, 113
Peter, George, **37**

pictographs and petroglyphs, 30-31
plants, 16, 18, 26, 27, 106, 111, 125, 126
Pollack, Jeff, 63, 65
pollution, 24
population, 41, 43, 46, 74
Portage, 37
Prairie du Chien, 37, 38, **38**
prairie grass, 18, 19

Racine, 20, 100, 109
reforestation, 24, 92, 99
Rhinelander, 115
Ringling Brothers Circus, 96, 135, 137
Ripon, 90, 91
rivers, 14, 125
Ryan, Buddy, 86

Salwey, Ken, 14, 16
sandstone formations, **20**, 118, 119
Schomer, Frank, 101
Schurz, Margarethe, 57, 135
service industries, 62, 69-70, 128
settlers, 20, 23, 24, 36, 39, 40, 41, 44
Shepard, Gene, 115
social welfare, 92
songs, 48-49, 113, 124
sports, 9, 70, 84-87, 107, 111
    fishing, 61-62, 70, 113, 117
    hiking, 16, 70, 119-120
    winter, 21, **22**, 70, 85, 114, 128-129
Spring Green, 120
statehood, 45, 123, 126
storytelling, 99, 100, 103, 113, 115

Thompson, Tommy, 9, 59, **60**, 81
Timms Hill, 13, 125

Topper, Tami, 96
tourism, 62, 70-71, 106-121, 128, 136-138
Tracy, Spencer, 94
transportation, 47, 92, 100-103, **101**, **103**, 136
trees, 16, 24, 25, 47, **50**, 111, 125

Vianden, Heinrich, **28-29**

wars, 84
waterfalls, 114
Watertown, 57
Waukesha, 109
West Allis, 109
White, Reggie, 86-87, **87**
Whitewater, 96
Wilder, Gene, 94
Wilder, Laura Ingalls, 98-99, 131
Wilder, Thornton, 98

wildlife refuge, 26, 118
Winnebago Indians, 32, **33**, **35**, 36, 41
Wisconsin Dells, 118, **119**
Wisconsin River, 14, **33**, 37, 125
wood and paper items, 47
Wright, Frank Lloyd, 120, 135

zoo, 106, 137